THE
HARD TRUTH
ABOUT
Soft-Selling

THE

HARD TRUTH

ABOUT

Soft-Selling

Restoring Pride & Purpose to the Sales Profession

George W. Dudley with Dr. John F. Tanner

The Hard Truth About Soft-Selling

Manufactured in the United States of America.

Publisher's Cataloging-in-Publication
(Provided by Quality Books, Inc.)
Dudley, George W., 1943-
The hard truth about soft-selling : restoring pride &
purpose to the sales profession / George W. Dudley with
John F. Tanner, Jr.
p. cm.
Includes bibliographical references and index.
LCCN 2005924402
ISBN-10: 0-935907-08-4 (HC)

1. Selling.   I. Tanner, John F. II. Title.
HF5438.25.D835 2005   658.85
                        QBI05-200129

1 2 3 4 5 6 7 8 9 10

Table of Contents

Preface

- In an eagerly anticipated speech, a well-known CEO advises a convention audience of senior managers, *"the overwhelming majority of ethics problems I've had to deal with come from people who talk about how much integrity they have. In our company, that's a red flag."*

- The author of a new sales book exhorts salespeople to sincerely care about their customers. Quoting venerable sales sage, Zig Ziglar, he writes: *"people don't care how much you know until they know how much you care."* The author's new book is: *The Science of Influence: How to Get Anyone to Say YES in 8 Minutes or Less.*

- In an effort to "elevate the ethical behavior of salespeople" a motivational speaker known for his impassioned speeches on the importance of principled selling offers an on-line *Sales Ethics Checklist.* The checklist was plagiarized from another website.

Values. Principles. Integrity. Virtues. Ethically, we live in an ironic age. U.S. president, Bill Clinton's wily assault on truth and meaning, Michael Moore's political bias artlessly touted as "documentary filmmaking" and high-minded mission statements brightening the hallways of organizations like Arthur Andersen and Enron have made people necessarily wary—if not cynical. In a sense, we seem to be drifting relentlessly downwards to, "a looser more skeptical relationship with the truth" (Stengel, 2000, p. 13).

Unspoken wariness is bound to flourish when the concept of truth itself becomes corrupted into just another flashy commercial offering, like "body language," to be colorfully presented by lavishly paid speakers at sales conventions (where copies of their presentations and training programs, slickly packaged into four gospel-like "modules," always seem to be conveniently available for purchase at the back of the auditorium).

Salespeople today are routinely indoctrinated in the black art of projecting the *appearance* of trust, warmth, sincerity and caring. The "sincerity industry" relentlessly pitches integrity and principles as if they were commodities and seems unmindful (and unbothered) by the inherent irony in *training* people to act sincere. Salespeople have understandably forgotten to ask: "*what is it about acting sincere that makes me sincere?*"

The driving purpose behind this book is to answer that question. The answer was, is and always will be: "nothing." Regardless of your sales setting, the presentational style you use, or the number of times buzzwords like "trust" "empathy" and "empowerment" are factored into your sales presentations, trustworthiness remains an ethical ideal grounded in honorable behavior. The formula has not changed. Honorable behavior still requires honorable *intent.*

No approach to selling has a monopoly on virtue. So it is not for us to favor one method while rejecting others. That is not our purpose. Doing so would only serve to liberate salespeople from one selling caste only to replace it with another. That said, we have not been reticent to charbroil those sales gurus who's proprietary preachments rant that salespeople who disagree with them are unprofessional, and as an afterthought, probably doomed to hell.

Selling is not inherently dishonest and salespeople need not disguise or apologize for their once-proud profession. Selling is no more or less honorable than any other profession and surely much more honorable than some. Like other professions, when selling is practiced with honor and skill, it does not require high-minded rhetoric, transparent excuses or ethical pretenses to be effective. Hopefully the pages that follow will provoke thoughtful discussion among sales professionals about the moral legitimacy of what they do and challenge their need to pretend to be doing anything other than selling.

We hope you enjoy reading this book. It is not a sales makeover and does not require you to change either your personality or your principles. The only prerequisites are an open mind and an inquisitive spirit.

George W. Dudley
Behavioral Sciences Research Press

John (Jeff) F. Tanner
Center for Professional Selling
Baylor University

Acknowledgements

Modestly sized books are usually intended to be "fast reads." Some are also enigmas, deceptively quick, informationally dense introductions to topics that can have important consequences. The first draft of *The Hard Truth About Soft-Selling* appeared over five years ago. Since then it has been subjected to intense fact checks, and the withering array of revisions necessary to craft a small book that is easily accessible to general readers and at the same time respectful of academic standards and conventions. That usually requires contributions from a lot of bright and creative people, and the *Hard Truth* is no exception.

The help and support provided by the research and administrative team at Behavioral Sciences Research Press in Dallas was invaluable. Alvin Ee, Belinda Gholston, Emmett Beam, Robert Ismert, Jeanne Ketchersid, Jacqueline Calder, John Goodson and Suzanne Dudley all provided much needed assistance. Behavioral Sciences' Senior Research Associate, Trelitha Bryant is due a "special thank you" for her expert assistance preparing and analyzing the data behind many of the empirical studies mentioned in this book. Terry Donia and Jeff Putnam provided helpful editing support and suggestions.

We would also like to thank Carol Ann Dudley, former senior research assistant (chemical senses and biochemistry departments, University of Texas Southwestern Medical School) for her insightful comments.

We would also like to thank members of Behavioral Sciences' Scientific Advisory Board who have had to sit through presentations of some of the supportive studies cited in this book. Insights gained from their intellectually vibrant criticisms and suggestions helped to shape the contour of this book though we would not presume upon their level of agreement with the specific content. Members are Dr. Howard Gershenfeld, Associate Professor of Psychiatry and Integrative Biology at the Univeristy of Texas Southwestern Medical School at Dallas; Dr. Ira H. Bernstein, Professor of Psychology, Department of Psychology, University of Texas at Arlington; Dr. Kebreten Manaye, Assistant Professor, Department of Physiology and Biophysics, Howard University College of Medicine, Washington, D.C.; Dr. Clive A. Fletcher, formerly Professor of Occupational Psychology at Goldsmiths' College, University of London, where he still holds the title of Emeritus Professor after leaving to work in private practice; and the late Dr. Douglas N. Jackson, former Professor of Psychology, University of Western Ontario, a distinguished scientist whose contributions continue to tower over the science of personality measurement.

Finally, this book would never have seen printer's ink if it had not been for the tenacious efforts of Behavioral Sciences' publisher and CEO, Shannon L. Goodson. Her personal encouragement (insistence) on meeting deadlines was only exceeded by her unwavering belief that the *Hard Truth About Soft-Selling* needed to be published. We are grateful for the many hours she spent personally writing, editing, and upgrading the content to the specifications needed for a coherent and effectively argued book. Practically speaking, there was a third author, and it was her.

"Surprisingly, instead of an army of sensitive, soft-spoken top producers, many organizations have increasingly found themselves saddled with a generation of confused, hesitant, over-trained, under producing professional visitors."

1

Welcome to the Soft-Sell Revolution

A new kind of sales training program emerged on the American business scene in the early 1970s. Touted as a revolutionary alternative to traditional "hard sell" sales approaches, these programs quickly found favor among battle-weary sales managers, eager to defeat what they perceived as long-standing negative attitudes toward the sales profession. Lured by promises of increased productivity, higher retention rates and happier salespeople, sales organizations everywhere began to abandon existing training structures in favor of this progressive new approach. The soft-sell revolution had begun.

Today, the transformation from traditional selling to a new soft and fuzzy way to sell is almost complete in the United States. Australia, New Zealand, the United Kingdom and several other countries are close behind and catching up quickly. Like statues of Lenin in the dying days of the Soviet Union, playright Arthur Miller's grinning, glad-handing icon, Willie Loman, has been toppled. In its place is a shiny new ideal of the successful salesperson: kinder, gentler, less self-interested, less manipulative, more empathetic.

Today, soft-selling and its new-sell variants have become the sales profession's wishing well, its Mardi Gras, its circus. The result is a massive, tectonic shift in attitudes, methods and intent away from closing and toward relating. But is the new paradigm a harbinger of good things to come, or merely wishful thinking?

The Unbearable Lightness of Soft-Selling

In the catchphrase-crazy sales profession, "soft-selling" stands out as a true ninety-day wonder: it's easy to remember, ripe with tantalizing connotations and trickier to pin down than Bill Clinton's definition of "sex." In this book "soft-selling" will be used to refer to the entire family of "client-centered," low-pressure sales approaches that have swept the sales profession during the last two decades. The soft-sell philosophy has been marketed successfully under a variety of names, including "consultative," "client-focused," "win-win," "relationship-based," and "solution-based" selling. Some are trademarked brand names representing specific book and workshop based training programs. Others have been more or less opportunistically attached to mass-produced "how-to" books for salespeople explaining, extolling and exploiting many of the generic general principles behind the selling reformation.

It is our intention to identify and dissect the new approach as a general selling style rather than any program in particular.

To do so, we drew from observations and conversations with many salespeople, managers and senior sales executives. We also examined a wide variety of soft-sell books that ran the gamut from national bestsellers to undersold, overstocked titles. All of them dipped into the same well of common themes and recurring buzzwords to make their points. But we didn't stop there. As you will see, we also reviewed appropriate academic texts and important scholarly journals for this book.

Chief among the shared characteristics of soft-sell programs are *non-evaluative* listening and *non-directive* relating. As you will see, these concepts now sanctified by soft-sell gurus actually come directly from approaches to psychotherapy developed in the 1950s, along with a generous serving of greeting card slogans like "developing empathy" and "creating congruence." With myriad variations, they comprise the conceptual core of soft-selling.

For the purpose of this investigation and to give a framework to readers who have been exposed to various combinations, contortions, permutations and outright Darwinian mutations of soft-selling, we suggest the following working definition of the soft-sell philosophy:

> *Soft-selling is a client-centered approach to sales in which the primary role of the seller is to create an atmosphere of trust and cooperation which enables the consumer to reach an informed buying decision free from pressure or manipulation.*

Reading between the lines of this seemingly innocuous definition, we can identify a number of implicit assumptions about the
"traditional" sales approaches that soft-selling was designed to
supplant. These assumptions represent a persistent subtext bubbling under the surface of most soft-sell texts. They include:

1. Traditional selling is primarily transaction oriented
   and places closing the sale above the needs of the
   client.

2. Traditional selling creates a mistrustful, adversarial
   relationship between buyer and seller.

3. In traditional selling, the buyer is pressured and
   intimidated into buying before he is ready or
   willing to do so.

Not content to rely on gently whispered subliminal messages, many soft-sell marketers today are far more explicit in
their evaluation of traditional selling practices. They brand
them all as "pushy," "manipulative," "old-fashioned" and
"ineffective." Unlike other sales training programs that aim
to *augment* your existing base of knowledge, skill and ability,
the soft-sell approach exhorts salespeople and sales managers
to create an entirely new framework for the selling process,
scrapping traditional notions of prospecting, presenting and
closing.

In exchange for this radical reshaping, soft-sell gurus
promise a profound transformation. Adopting their approach,
they claim, will demolish the stereotypical image of the salesperson as a slick, fast-talking, manipulative hustler. Trust
and rapport will become the bedrock of successful selling, as

opposed to high-pressure tactics and intimidation. By allowing the sale to flow naturally from the forthright exchange of information and the parallel development of a mutually rewarding business relationship, sales will increase dramatically. The needs of both the buyer and the seller will be fulfilled in an atmosphere of mutual respect and cooperation.

It certainly *sounds* revolutionary. But has it worked? Has the revolution lived up to its claims?

That depends on how you look at it. From the financial standpoint of the gurus tallying sales of their respective books, tapes and training programs, soft-selling has been an unqualified success.

Self-help book-of-the-week authors know that every technique, no matter how trivial, works for *somebody*. Naturally, for some salespeople and some companies, soft-selling has proven beneficial. You can't argue with success, even spurious success, and we don't intend to. In the hotly competitive markets of the early 21st century and beyond, any sales philosophy that produces positive results deserves to be respectfully acknowledged, if not embraced.

With its new techniques, the vocabulary of soft-selling has infiltrated the standard sales and marketing lexicon of our time—to the extent that one financial services giant now boasts in its advertisements, "We invest in *relationships*." Customers have become conditioned to expect a different kind of relationship with salespeople and the entire training and development industry has scrambled to reflect the change in attitudes toward buying and selling. Now, even many so-called "traditional" sales development programs garnish their training with stylistic topics like "rapport" and "professionalism."

Dazzled by promises and visions of a golden future, an entire generation of businesses has gamely attempted to implement the soft-sell approach. Always searching for the latest competitive edge, many hard-working salespeople uncritically swallowed the soft-sell philosophy—whole. As a result, the corporate landscape is now dotted with sales organizations that wouldn't dream of simply advocating their products to prospective buyers, of talking when they could be listening, or closing before they fully "validated" themselves and their product.

Soft-Sell Utopia?

All, however, may not be well. Scratch the surface and this client-centered Utopia may really be the opposite—Dystopia. From the depths of some sales departments we have begun to hear tentative, subterranean whispers: despite a surplus of rapport and empathy, *soft-selling salespeople are not selling more.* Surprisingly, instead of an army of sensitive, soft-spoken top producers, many organizations have increasingly found themselves saddled with a generation of confused, hesitant, over-trained, under-producing *professional visitors.* Today's "product advisors" (please don't call them "salespeople") have gained impressive insights into the minds of prospective customers—but they may have lost sight of the "bottom line." Many, confused and conflicted about what salespeople are supposed to be and do, are trapped in the sales profession's equivalent of the twilight zone.

So beware. Testimonials are not evidence; inferences are not proof. For two decades now, without evidence and largely without dissent, soft-selling marketers have persistently offered up their approach as the panacea for the "ills" of traditional selling. It isn't. In fact, we've found that in *some* industries and for *some* salespeople, soft-selling can actually do more harm than good. However, you won't hear that from the leaders of the soft-selling revolution whose charismatic exhortations sometimes verge on demagoguery. To them, soft-selling is infallible and, like a rising tide, will inevitably succeed in washing away all challenges to its supremacy.

But every revolution has dissenters. We've chosen to take on that role—not to try to undermine soft-selling, but simply to lend some balance and, we hope, some perspective to what has been a markedly one-sided pitch. Our objective is clear. We want salespeople, their managers, trainers and employers to stop, pause for a moment, and think about what they are doing, how they are doing it, and why. There is a massive amount of "mythinformation" about sales psychology in circulation. It's time to take a calm, dispassionate look at the theory—and the reality—of the new, softer approach to selling.

What does soft-selling mean? Is there an alternative? Are there messages implicit in the philosophy that you should examine? Let's ask hard questions. Search for answers. Demand meaningful evidence. Become knowledgeable irritants. It's your profession. It's your career.

It's not our intention to convert you to any particular selling approach—soft, hard or otherwise. One author is a research scientist who specializes in the development of diagnostic and remedial psychological assessments for salespeople and studies the similarities and differences of salespeople around the world. The other, a professor, is an academic scholar who teaches and publishes formal studies related to the sales profession and the people in it. Frankly, we don't care which sales training philosophy you use or do not use. That's your call. We simply want you, like any other professional, to understand your choices.

"Soft-selling emits an ennobling, altruistic aura on the order of missionary work among the poor…"

2

Origins of the Soft-Sell Revolution

The $35 billion-per-year training and development industry is a trend-obsessed monster. Fads come and go with all the affectations and fickleness of Paris fashions. Year after year, human resources and training departments search for the latest ways to orient, inform and entertain employees, while shrewd marketing gurus take note of what's hot now and rack their brains to create the Next Big Thing.

Will it be left-brain/right-brain theories? Re-engineering? Will subliminal messages re-emerge again as they tend to do about every five years? What about the virtual corporation? Viagra for the mind? Or, perhaps it will be yet another variation of those simplistic four-part grid assessments which attempts to condense five billion human beings down to four or five personality trait combinations? The neon array of sales-boosting offerings available worldwide resembles the super-market cereal aisle: infinite varieties of colorful, aggressively marketed product—all essentially derived from the same four basic grains.

Sales training has become a thriving subspecialty of the training industry. Given the astronomical turnover rate in some sales-driven industries and the escalating cost of replacing salespeople, it's not surprising that new programs and "experts" surface weekly. They're easy to spot anxiously working the hallways of sales conferences and conventions like predators in search of their next meal. Their target? A piece of the lucrative and apparently insatiable market for "surefire" sales boosting programs. Or spend a few minutes (or less) looking around in the feverish, overcrowded sales training ghetto on the World Wide Web. Prospecting, presenting, negotiating, client tracking, closing and servicing—all receive manic attention from marketing mavens claiming to hold the exclusive secret to great sales success. Perhaps the perpetual urgency of the sales training market can be understood by an estimate: According to some studies it can cost from US $100,000 to upwards of a million dollars in recruiting, training and lost income to replace a non-producing salesperson who never should have been hired in the first place (Churchill, Ford, & Walker, 1990; Gilbert, 2004). And that figure fails to account for the loss of market repute that can place an artificially low ceiling on an organization's ability to competitively attract future sales talent (Dudley,1981).

From the beginning of the soft-sell movement, its proponents have worked hard to differentiate their philosophy from the overcrowded sales training pack. It isn't just a new way to sell, they declare, but (cue fanfare) *a total restructuring of the selling paradigm.* No long-held assumption about selling escapes scrutiny and subsequent reassessment, from "why do customers buy?" to "what's the 'correct' outcome of a sales presentation?" If you think it's a signed purchase order, you're hopelessly mired in what one author derisively calls "Oldsell" (Hewitt-Gleeson,1990). One guidebook even presents its program as "a new approach to *exchange*," as if the pedestrian word *selling* is no longer adequate to describe the revolutionary forces at work (Plotkin,1995).

Revolutions have to start somewhere, yet, most adherents of the soft-sell approach are unaware of its origins. Now that soft-sell programs have been warmly embraced and widely adopted, loyal followers uncritically accept the marketeer's party line: that soft-selling originated from market research which indicated that overwhelmingly negative attitudes towards salespeople were causing people to buy less and salespeople to sell less. While that scenario may contain an element of truth, it implies that the soft-sell philosophy was a unique, spontaneous response to attitudes held by the general public about salespeople. But, the truth is out there. And, it's more interesting and considerably more instructive than that.

Is soft-selling really the complete facelift, as its gurus promise, or merely a cosmetic makeover? Move over, Estee Lauder®! Authentic revolutions are infrequent when it comes to sales training. "Breakthroughs" are often little more than re-packaged material from years past or "borrowed" content from other professions. Soft-selling is no exception. While its high priests may boldly proclaim its unique and innovative qualities, it actually guards a dirty little secret: innovation is not theirs to claim. The situation is not without humor because the current crop of sales coaches and "experts" don't seem to realize that their programs are faded copies of original ideas derived from an unlikely source entirely outside of sales training.

In the 1960s, Xerox® developed the granddaddy of modern soft-sell programs, Professional Selling Skills (PSS). A promotional piece, which categorically touted PSS as "the world's leading sales training program," defined success as

> . . . *abandoning high-pressure sales tactics and adopting a more consultative approach to selling. The objective: to build customer trust and rapport and help your salespeople differentiate themselves—and your services or products—in a crowded marketplace.*

According to their brochure, more than two million salespeople benefited from their program. Effectiveness? It's there if you want it to be, but it looks like a shell game. A "Participant Attitude Questionnaire," a "Seminar Quality Checklist" for the instructor to fill out, and a "Mastery Test" for the participant to complete and self-score are the only means included under "Measurement" in the brochure's bullet listings. No guidance is provided, for example, to conduct meaningful pre/post studies to verify actual increases in sales production as a result of the training.

A few years later, Larry Wilson—an insurance agent turned training guru—polished up some of the same concepts and principles and packaged them into the first aggressively marketed soft-sell package which was titled "Counselor Selling." Ever versatile, Wilson has since moved on through other things, including a pop-psych program called "Connecting With People" and an experiential learning retreat for businesspeople similar to Outward Bound®. More recently, Wilson Learning has re-engineered a new version of the Counselor Selling program entitled "The Counselor Salesperson" which is essentially soft-selling with a new twist. "Taking a counselor approach to sales is about understanding 'the business of the business' so you can help customers solve real business problems . . .[it] enables salespeople to differentiate themselves by demonstrating that they have what it takes to help execute business strategy, not just make another sale" (Wilson Learning, 2001).

But even these two early efforts at creating a "new" approach to sales can trace their roots back at least two decades earlier to a common genetic ancestor—one which is all but ignored now, but whose influence spread like burning embers across the modern sales training landscape.

Many of the beliefs, methods and even language of Carl Rogers' "client-centered" approach to psychotherapy are at the core of the soft-sell revolution. Rogers was the intellectual mentor to the "encounter group" movement of the 1960s. Client-centered psychology was developed in reaction to the Freudian psychoanalysis then prevalent. Rogers (1942) first made his approach to therapy explicit in his book *Counseling and Psychotherapy*. As he later explained in his classic work *Client-Centered Therapy*, he believed that if you create the right problem-solving conditions, people will find their own solutions (Rogers, 1951). Those "right" conditions included a "nondirective, nonjudgmental" environment and a trusting, empathic relationship between therapist and client. Familiar soft-sell concepts such as "unconditional positive regard" and "reflective listening" were lifted directly from Rogers' work.

Also, soft-sellers today use the term "client," rather than more plainspoken terms such as "consumer," "customer," "shopper," or "buyer."

> ***Q:*** *Is Rogerian therapy the one where you ask a straightforward question and they won't answer but only reflect or paraphrase back to you what you asked?*
>
> ***A:*** *You want to know if Rogerian therapy is the one where when you ask a straightforward question they won't answer but only reflect or paraphrase back to you what you asked?*
>
> ***Q:*** *That's what I said, isn't it? What's the matter with you can't you hear?*
>
> ***A:*** *You feel there's something wrong with me, and that I can't hear?*

In client-centered "rent-a-friend" shrink shops, the therapist assumed responsibility for establishing a warm, accepting relationship with clients. Therapists were expected to project empathy, congruence and non-judgmental warmth so completely that ". . . An 'empathic' therapist perceives the experience of the client with such accuracy that he might almost be the client" (Campbell,1994, p. 73). To clients, congruent therapists were absolutely and unconditionally sincere and genuine. According to the research examining the effectiveness of these conditions, such interpersonal factors were essential for the psychotherapy to be successful and the goals of emotional awareness and growth to be achieved.

Rogers' client-centered system was the first major psychotherapy to originate in the United States. Naturally, it reflected many of the parochial customs and beliefs at the core of American culture. For example, Rogers insisted that therapists relate to their patients as equals. However egalitarian this sounds, using the term "client" often masked a therapist's condescension and smugness which "has to do with power and pretension to knowledge" (Baker,1996, p. 154).

Client-centered therapy has not fared particularly well over the years. "Competent therapists," says one commentator,

> . . . *realize that while such a relationship is necessary, it is rarely sufficient to foster the resolution of client distress. Effective therapy is more than an 'art.' Clients in therapy should be able to expect legitimately effective services. They should not have to endure some free-form emotional experience at the hands of a self-appointed artist (Campbell, 1994, p. 78).*

With the possible exception of licensed mental health counselors (formerly affiliated with the American Personnel and Guidance Association), client-centered psychotherapists have been left to empathetically reflect on their own inadequacies. Clinically oriented psychologists and psychiatrists have migrated to modern cognitive behavioral treatment modalities. But if you would like to explore the Rogerian origins of soft-selling further, go to any university library. There's plenty of source material still readily available—easily accessible, light (but, to be honest, tedious) reading.

The notion of introducing a rapport-based, problem-solving approach to a profession chronically dogged by accusations of high-pressure peddling has understandable appeal. Yet, modern soft-sell gurus seem blissfully unaware of, and therefore completely unperturbed by, the origin of their pet philosophy. According to veteran behavioral scientist Shannon L. Goodson (personal communication, March 31, 1999), co-author of the international bestseller *The Psychology of Sales Call Reluctance* (Dudley, G.W. & Goodson, S.L., 1999):

> *Rogerian concepts are ideals, not principles. They describe what people could be like in a perfect world. But, they are completely incompatible with, and inappropriate to, the context of real-world selling—which is, by definition, outcome-oriented. In my opinion, when they are a featured part of sales training, the damage these Rogerian concepts inflict on salespeople is incalculable and inexcusable.*

When the first soft-sellers imported Rogerian theories into their sales training models, a critical nuance was lost in the translation. The client-centered approach may be effective as a *psychotherapy*—and even that is the subject of heated debate among professionals—but it was never intended for application to sales. To work, non-directive therapy requires a great deal of time, a great deal of patience, and *absolute willingness* on the part of the therapist to refrain from nudging or prompting. That's not selling. That's . . . well, *therapy*. Applying client-centered techniques to sales may be a novel idea, but it's hardly what Rogers had in mind when he introduced his approach.

Non-directive Selling in the Real World?

Just imagine. You're in a prospect's office. You have five minutes—maybe—to impress this person with the features, benefits, cost and value of your product or service. You need this sale to make your monthly quota. And the prospect already thinks your competitor's product is just dandy. Oh yes . . . and you're not supposed to ask leading questions or try to influence the prospect's behavior in any way. Ready? Sell.

The respective goals of selling and therapy are simply different. Rogers developed client-centered therapy as a way to increase personal insight, not to produce a signature on a purchase order.

But that's not the only reason to question the transformation of client-centered psychotherapy of the 1950s into the soft-selling revolution of today. Are the practical skills transferable to selling? Soft-selling programs presume that the same techniques used in client-centered therapy to solve an individual's personal problems will work equally well for solving customer's business problems. Unfortunately, without hard evidence to the contrary, that's a bit like assuming a barber will make a good surgeon.

That's just what happened in the Middle Ages, when the town barber was also the town sawbones. Originally, barbers assisted priests and monks, who were the surgeons. After all, they reasoned that a knife was a knife, and if you could shave someone's face without cutting his throat surely you could make an incision down his middle and peer inside. Thankfully, it later became clear that the skills required to cut someone's hair and save a soul were not as transferable as previously thought, and surgery developed into a separate discipline requiring many years of specialized training.

It should be equally obvious that a salesperson cannot simply step into a psychotherapist's shoes. Don't feel bad; most therapists couldn't perform well in a sales job either. Despite some superficial similarities exploited by soft-sellers, the two professions are not interchangeable, and neither are the techniques, training, and the skill level required to achieve their respective goals.

Further, not only is the client-centered approach questionable in sales, it is no longer considered applicable in psychotherapy. A half-century later, Rogers' approach remains controversial and has largely fallen out of favor. Some of the newer cognitive behavioral approaches to therapy like Rational Emotive Behavior Therapy popularized by Albert Ellis (1970) (where the self-talk craze originated) and Aaron Beck's Cognitive Therapy (1976), originally developed as a response by the psychological community to widespread dissatisfaction with rambling, time-consuming, non-directive Rogerian therapy (Gross, 1978). One critic of client-centered therapy has raised doubts about who actually benefited from the empathic approach:

> *Though their demeanor is relatively benevolent, CC-H (client-centered-humanist) therapists are not necessarily more sensitive to what their clients need. Additionally, the kind and gentle appearance of CC-H therapists can be deceptive. They impose their agenda on clients as often as therapists of other orientations, but they exercise their authority more indirectly (Campbell, 1994, p. 123).*

Not surprisingly, the same implied criticism can be fairly leveled against soft-selling.

Radical Chic

The problematic paternity of soft-selling hasn't deterred its advocates from aggressively trumpeting the benefits of the client-centered approach. Inconsistencies notwithstanding, they have annointed it the First Commandment of soft-selling.

> *Selling requires the discipline of always thinking from the customer's viewpoint . . . (Schneider, 1990, p. vii).*

> *Your main motivation is to create value for your customers or clients . . . (Willingham, 1987, p. 71).*

> *Management must not expect salespeople to be result-oriented individuals but rather to be customer-driven professionals (Hewitt-Gleeson, 1990, p. 58).*

At first glance, these are simply spiffed-up refrains of the oldest of cherished retail bromides, "The customer is always right." On this level, we couldn't agree more. Your customers are your lifeblood. Without people to sell to, the superiority of your products and the polish of your presentations are meaningless—merely investments without return. In some highly competitive industries, there is so little differentiation in product and price from company to company that value-added considerations such as caring service and dedicated problem solving often represent the deciding factor in the customer's decision to buy from you—or one of your competitors. That is as it should be.

Nowadays only the most shortsighted sales training programs neglect the fundamentals of good customer service. As a concept to build a selling revolution around, it seems self-evident, almost simplistic. But soft-selling doesn't stop there. It stretches the idea of customer-friendly selling beyond its practical limits—and then some. According to the gurus, to fully embrace soft-selling, you must become *radically client-centered*—instead of *sales-centered.*

"Fulfilling the prospective client's needs with outstanding service [must] replace making a sale no matter what," proclaims one radically client-centered training program (Johnston & Withers, 1992, p. xii). Not accompany. Not supplement. *Replace.* An Australian sales training expert with the same mindset echoes the sentiment: "In 'New Sell' (the proprietary brand of soft-selling he markets), the salesperson is more interested in the *process* than the result" (Hewitt-Gleeson, 1990, p. 37).

The idea that the buyer-seller *relationship* is more important than the *sale* strikes us as absurd and counterproductive. Like most relativistic attempts to make all sides equal and all opinions mere matters of taste or preference, the argument eventually collapses under the weight of its own inescapable self-contradiction.

It's perfectly possible, if not necessarily desirable, to close a sale without developing any kind of rapport with a customer whatsoever. But what about the flip side? Can you strike up a relationship without closing a sale? And if you can do so, should you? There's a limit to the number of expense-account lunches that most sales organizations will approve without demonstrable progress toward a deal. Clearly a different set of assumptions about the goal of selling is at work here.

And so it is. In adopting a radically client-centered orientation, soft-selling created an entirely new dogma about the real goal of selling. "Burn this into your brain," warns one author. "Selling isn't selling, it's need-fulfillment" (Willingham, 1987, p.26). See the difference? If you allow that statement to stand as fact, then any straightforward exchange of your goods for the customer's money becomes an inefficient, unimaginative, even discourteous use of selling resources. In soft-selling, you must be much more than simply a cog in the mechanism of supply and demand. Only when your client's needs are uncovered, explored and evaluated can the prosaic matter of *selling* be broached.

Soft-selling advocates also have a ready explanation for the problem they call "relationship tension" in traditional selling. It is, these experts say, unseemly power-tripping which happens because you (the seller) have something the other guy (the buyer) wants. To correct this inequity, according to the client-centered gurus, all the seller needs to do is put the customer firmly in the driver's seat. "Product-centered selling (the old way) is 'pushy.' Customer-centered selling isn't 'pushy,' because the customer's objectives determine the sale" (Schneider, 1990, p. viii).

Under these circumstances, in soft-selling it is incumbent on the salesperson to meet all of the buyer's criteria for making a purchase, *whatever they are*. While this semantic tweaking may reduce the likelihood of you being considered a boorish hustler, one can only hope that client-centered hostage negotiation manuals don't appear on bookstore shelves any time soon, or digital person-centered watches which display whatever time you need it to be.

Relationship Reality Check

When we were kids, some of us believed that if we buttered up the school bully and cheerfully coughed up our lunch money on demand, he would be our pal. It rarely worked then, and it doesn't work now. Soft-selling erroneously assumes that customers will automatically buy from the individual or company who treats them best. Sometimes it happens that way. But sometimes, despite your best efforts, the customer will accept your free lunches and your valuable consulting time—and still buy from your competitor for reasons that have nothing to do with the warm relationship you've established.

That's why, in the final analysis, you can't depend on relationship-building skills alone to make the sale for you. Hone those skills and make them work for you. But don't confuse making friends with making sales. Your company won't. Regardless of what they say in their advertising, when was the last time your employers paid you a "friendship bonus?"

In short, the radical client-centered orientation cleverly refashions the sales sphere as a Utopian marketplace in which you play benevolent sales genie, granting your customer's fondest wishes with a deep bow and an ultra sincere smile. Men and women behave like angels. Customer service ceases to be merely a better means to a more profitable end and becomes a career-defining end in itself. Closing a sale may be a happy consequence of your high-minded sales actions from time to time, but it's never a goal worthy of pursuit for its own sake.

Undiluted soft-selling emits an ennobling, altruistic aura on the order of missionary work among the poor. Here the brooks ripple, the air is clean, birds sing Mozart, and everyone wants to be a salesperson. Single-handedly, soft-selling is transforming the entire sales profession into an appealing, stress-free Disneyland®. No matter how desperate one may be to believe such fantasies, these are scenarios that do not—cannot—accurately portray the reality of selling in a competitive market.

Fortunately, a few notable sales coaches have managed to preserve 20/20 sales training vision in a world blurred by soft-selling. Alfred Tack (1993) saw it this way:

*[T]he object of a salesman at every interview is to persuade
. . . [H]owever long the salesman has known the buyer,
however friendly the relationship between them, the salesman has to use selling skills if he is to persuade the buyer
to place an order (p. 14).*

U.K. sales expert John Fenton (1984) adds:

*The only reason a Seller is employed is to get orders. The
only logical reason for a meeting between a Buyer and
Seller is to give and receive and order—if not now, at
some definable time in the near future (p. 249).*

Writing about complex sales involving large, multi-sector
organizations, Heiman and Sanchez (1998) advocate a practical, balanced perspective:

*In a complex sales arena, you have short-term and long-
term objectives. In the short term, you want to close as
many individual pieces of business as you can. In the long
term, you want to maintain healthy relations with the
customers signing for these deals, so that they'll be willing
to make further purchases from you in the months and
years to come (p. 48).*

Anthony Parinello (1999), author of *Selling to VITO* says:

*... today's salespeople have to produce more, faster, and
find more new business than the salespeople of ten or
twenty years ago....They're being told, 'Keep us ahead of
the competition' (p. 7).*

Finally, venerable sales trainer Brian Tracy (1993) reminds salespeople that one of the seven core requirements of selling is obtaining commitment:

> *[The] ability to . . . obtain commitment to take action is the endgame of selling. If you do everything well except for this, you will still fail (p. 174).*

Burn *this* into your brain: Selling *is* selling. A salesperson's job is not merely to fulfill customers' needs. It is to *sell* them the product or service that can help fulfill their needs. Need-fulfillment, wish-fulfillment, will-fulfillment, and other intangible warm fuzzies are the currency of advertising, not selling.

According to a popular college textbook about selling, it costs 10,000 times more to reach potential customers via personal face-to-face selling than with a television ad (Weitz, Castleberry, & Tanner, 2004). Given the enormous cost involved, why would any corporation bother to marshal a personal selling force in this age of mass communication? Simple. While a well-produced commercial may be memorable, entertaining, and image-enhancing, it can't close a sale. Advertising can create a positive mental relationship between a customer and a product, but it can't ask for the order. And while millions of people may see a television commercial, the number who actually buy as a direct result is substantially smaller and, furthermore, unknowable. A salesperson with a specified quota and a realistic "hit" ratio takes the sales process out of the realm of psychobabble and places it in the land of bottom line accountability.

In Real World 101, in addition to meeting your customer's objectives, your professional objective as the seller must remain the same: to close the sale. If it's not, you're wasting your time. You're wasting your company's resources. And, you may be doing your clients a grave disservice.

Being radically client-centered strips you and your customers of your value as a knowledgeable product advocate. It reduces you to the level of a professional sycophant—a walking laugh track, capable of cheerfully saying only what your clients want to hear. Your relationships with your customers are too important for that. In this day of interchangeable products and cutthroat price wars, they're more important than ever. Your customers deserve better, and so do you.

If your *primary responsibility* is to close sales, building relationships cannot be your most important objective. Any selling technique you employ must be either *sales-advocating* and therefore not truly *client-centered*, or client-centered, and therefore not truly sales-advocating. Soft-selling claims to be both and winds up being neither.

"Successful selling is not attributable to any one style, taste, or preference. Period."

3

The Lexicon
of Soft-Selling

Let's pause at this point to define some of the buzzwords that soft-sell marketing gurus are using to create a favorable picture of their sales strategy.

Industrial Strength "Sincerity"

"Sincerity," "integrity" and "empathy" are ten-dollar words in the lexicon of soft-selling. Without them, say the gurus, your selling is doomed to be product-bound, manipulative and pushy.

Many soft-sell programs teach salespeople that they will increase sales if they *act* like their prospects' best friend. The market-friendly name for this technique is "building rapport." Ironically, some soft-sellers recommend all kinds of artful schemes to accomplish it. One text urges you to "create the similarities that build trust and minimize sales resistance . . . If what you're doing with a customer isn't working, try something else until you get the response you want—*anything* else" (Schneider, 1990, p. 71).

To paraphrase Abraham Lincoln, you can empathize with *some* of the people *all* of the time, and *all* of the people *some* of the time. But surely, *no one* can experience genuine empathy with *every* customer *every* time. What are you supposed to do when empathy just isn't possible? Fake it?

Apparently. The concept of universal empathy has spawned an entire cottage industry dedicated to teaching the dubious skill of manufacturing emotions on demand. We call it the *sincerity industry*. This enterprising sub-group of success gurus devotes itself to divulging simplistic tricks that mimic trustworthy, confidence-inspiring behaviors—without the muss and fuss of actually being trustworthy or confidence-inspiring.

A British advertisement for a book (Davies, 1995) on the subject reads in part, "You can *reproduce* [italics added] all the right signs in yourself to appear confident. And it is that *appearance* [italics added] of confidence that attracts all the benefits—the respect, the admiration, the co-operation, the trust, the belief in you." Best of all, assures the writer of this remarkable text, "There is no need to change your personality overnight." What a relief.

The Lexicon of Soft-Selling
"Selling"–What's in a Name?

"Relationship-building" is a popular soft-sell theme. The very phrase drips sweetly with connotations of trust and bonhomie. After all, you might rip off a stranger, but never someone with whom you had built a *relationship*. Would you?

To repeatedly assert that "selling is relationship-building" invests the sales process with so much warm and fuzzy surplus meaning that you may find yourself believing that's *all* selling is. But all kinds of occupations include relationship-building such as teaching, counseling, medicine, clergy, politics, management, social work, the practice of law, to name a few. Clearly, selling is more than just relationship-building. But, how much more? We aren't sure.

We are sure that selling is an inexact science. Actually, despite what some pundits will tell you, it's not a science at all. It's a hands-on trial-and error discipline practiced by diverse, unpredictable human beings and, therefore, not easily standardized, explained or consigned to the rigors of scientific research. A steadily accumulating number of scientific studies have attempted to quantify certain aspects of the selling process. However, the formal study of selling still seems to be considered the Yugo of scientific research by mainstream scientists working in other fields. Plainly, it's not neurophysiology or astrophysics.

Most scientific research fails to produce clear or expected results. Like the poker-playing wildcatters searching the oil fields of Texas and Oklahoma in 1900, the typical mainstream scientist sinks a lot of holes in hopes of finding one, great, nobel-winning gusher. Most never do. In our own case, the majority of properly designed sales studies using "noisy" real world data (rather than laboratory controls or simulations with students) have produced few decisive outcomes. Most only yield tormenting ambiguities in need of further research. When we do get results, they often fail to support our original hypothesis altogether, or worse yet, wind up contradicting the clear cut results produced by last week's experiments. Research is like that. Weekly scientific breakthroughs that promise to change the course of civilization are the stuff of lurid websites and television infomercials.

As a result, there are no widely accepted or established psychological laws governing the makeup of salespeople. Most "lawful" findings cannot bear the heat of objective verification and turn out to be little more than weightless theories, *Chicken Soup for the Soul*. There is no single widely agreed upon definition of what selling is. That's why so many sales training gurus have jumped on the bandwagon with their ready-to-market definitions. They don't have to bear the burden of producing systematic proof to support their "theories."

In this regard, erudite phrases, over-psychologized concepts and so-called "process" definitions substitute nicely. Thus, soft-sell purveyors have sold us "definitive" descriptions of selling:

- "Effective selling is simply good communication" (Johnston & Withers, 1992, p. 7).

- "Selling is influencing people by developing relationships and solving customer problems so there's a mutual exchange of value" (Schneider, 1990, p. 103).

- "Selling . . . is simply an exercise in human relationships" (Harle, 1990, p. v.).

- "Selling on Purpose is an intention, a way of life, the philosophy from which you operate. It's caring" (Johnson & Wilson, 1984, p. 28).

- "[Selling] requires investing a great deal of effort in manipulating and controlling the consciousness of others" (Lerner, 1995, p. 13).

For better or worse, selling is clearly all of these things—to a point. And, that is the point. Most successful salespeople are probably already good communicators, skilled problem-solvers, etc. But these contrived, trumped-up definitions are like slogans found on billboards, slickly designed web sites and those ubiquitous plastic pens with a company's name etched on them. By themselves, slogans don't sell anything. They are selling *tools*. They can help you sell more. *But they won't do your selling for you.*

For proof, you only need to consult your memory. Have you (or any salesperson you know) ever received a communication bonus? Have you ever been paid a commission on the amount of rapport you achieved with a client? Or, the number of new friends you made last year? Or the number of needs you uncovered and explored? Too often, the soft-selling fraternity would have you believe that selling is merely a matter of having the right tools.

Functionally speaking, **successful selling is what gets salespeople rewarded (paid in the form of commissions and bonuses) when they do it, and punished (sacked) when they don't.**

Granted, this definition is not ultra-psychological. It's definitely not sexy, and probably not "deep" enough to build a marketable training program around. But we like it because it's easy to understand and is perfectly clear. Successful salespeople close sales.

Our definition can create a nasty dilemma for soft-sell wizards who define "success" by using verbal gratuities such as attaining "rapport," "unconditional trust" and "active listening skills." Yet, in our studies we've encountered many highly successful salespeople who are, to put it bluntly, curmudgeonly SOBs. They may be an endangered species, but they are not rare. In terms of their "interpersonal skills" these Very High Producers have the appeal of a five-day-old loaf of bread, but still manage to earn annual commissions in the six figures. They may be unpleasant, even annoying, but their presence helps retain perspective and remind us of reality. Success in sales means getting things sold (that's self-evident), and successful selling is not attributable to any one style, taste or preference. Period.

The Lexicon of Soft-Selling "Professional"

"Professionalism" is a favorite buzzword of the gurus. They use it to entice unsuspecting salespeople the same way Charles Atlas enticed skinny kids with scenes of newly buffed ex-nerds kicking sand in the bully's face. "We've got the key to becoming something you're currently not," they whisper seductively. "Our sales approach will make you a *professional*."

For better or worse, that is a powerful come-on to many salespeople. According to popular perception, professionalism equals trust. And, historically trustworthiness has been lacking in the public's image of salespeople.

Seeing your occupation perennially appear near the bottom of the annual lists of "most trusted professions" takes its toll, consciously or unconsciously. Under siege by negative cultural stereotypes about sleazy salespeople (often perpetuated not just by the media but by friends, relatives and even sales management), it's very tempting to reach out to sympathetic training gurus who promise to confer "professional" status for the price of a book, a DVD or workshop.

On the subject of professionalism, soft-sellers tend to fall into two camps. There are those who smoothly assure you that you're not slippery and untrustworthy. It's just that your occupation puts you in the regrettable position of having to do slippery, untrustworthy things. Things like selling. Fortunately for you, they have the perfect solution. As suggested by one program teaching soft-selling to lawyers, consultants, etc. who wish to promote their businesses (i.e., sell their services), "They can try 'relationship selling,' which is ideal for them. This kind of selling can be learned easily, and is one they as *professionals* [italics added] will feel comfortable with" (Johnston & Withers, 1992, p.1).

Then there are gurus who shrug cynically, "So you're a manipulative, unsavory salesperson. You know it. I know it. Your customers know it. *But I can help you conceal it.*" This kind of "expert" promises that, using his techniques, "your selling will take on a new professionalism,"—presumably one that was utterly lacking before you became a soft-selling machine.

Let's pause here to demystify this provocative label. "Professional" is one of those highly malleable words whose connotation exceeds the scope of its literal meaning. The dictionary definition refers to being "worthy of the high standards of a *profession*"—profession being used generally to distinguish primarily cerebral occupations from manual labor. Suggested synonyms run the gamut from "skilled" and "trained" to "conscientious," "businesslike" and "authoritative."

In practice, "professional" can refer to an athlete who makes a living playing a game, or to members of certain occupations requiring a great deal of specialized education and training, such as physicians or architects. It can also refer to conduct that meets strict guidelines for honesty, fairness and detachment—often as verbal shorthand for "ethical." We suspect it's this latter definition that was the impetus for the recently popular "professional certification" movement in sales training.

Even among members of the sales community there is some dissension about the appropriateness of applying this rather amorphous word to the business of selling. One critic of the certification process recently worried that, merely by setting it up as a standard to be attained, the word professional, "once a dignified accolade for worthies like doctors and lawyers has become ghettoized and cheesy" (Nylen, 1996, p. 70).

Using their usual modus operandi, soft-sell marketers have pounced on this definitional dilemma and turned it to their advantage. To whet your appetite for their "professional" techniques, they subtly encourage your belief in the stereotypical image of the unprofessional salesperson—not merely as an archetype, but as a personal identification.

We don't claim to have the last word in this debate. It will surely continue to swirl around the edges of the training industry like dust on a cattle drive. We would like to go on record as believing that professional conduct is within the grasp of any hard-working individual. So is unprofessional conduct. But making sales your career choice does not fatalistically mire you in a swamp of dishonor. With rare exceptions, professionalism is not something conferred upon you by virtue of the line of work you've chosen. And, it's not a quality that can be automatically bestowed or withheld by *any* sales training program, or organization, no matter what the gurus say.

"Despite the uncompromising claims of soft-sell gurus, dishonesty and "hustling" are not integral components of traditional selling. They never have been."

4

The Hard Line of Soft-Selling

Soft-selling programs trumpet their jargon—"flexibility" and "nonjudgmentality," "versatile," "objective" and "unbiased" as watchwords of success. Anything else is rigid and won't fly. They have a new paradigm. ("Paradigm" is yet another one of those overworked words "which few modern philosophers [take] seriously anymore" (Horgan, 1996, p. 56)). According to physicist Thomas Kuhn who is credited with popularizing the term in *The Structure of Scientific Revolutions*, the word is "hopelessly out of control," spreading "like a virus . . . [until it has come] to signify any dominant idea" (Horgan, 1996, p 45).

One author dependent on buzzwords goes so far as to admonish readers, "All you are trying to sell is your objectivity" (Hewitt-Gleeson, 1990, p 55). This Zen-like mantra neatly sums up the soft-sell concept of the *organic sale*, in which you, the salesperson, are more or less a spiritual guide accompanying buyers down the path of free choice. It's downright Buddhist. (But, if you sell your objectivity, is it gone forever, or does it come back to you later?)

Client-centered selling, its gurus preach, requires near-complete submission to the needs of individual customers in order to achieve "congruence." Once a simple mathematical term signifying "agreement," soft-sellers have lately imbued "congruence" with profound psychological meaning. "Canned" sales presentations, which treat all customers uniformly, are out. So are presumptions about what prospective buyers really want without first probing their deepest needs and desires. According to one marketing consultant, "To be successful, the Rainmaker must first get to the essence, the *core* [italics added], of what the customer needs.... The Rainmaker must understand all of the customer's concerns, desires, fears, and limits" (Fox, 2000, p. 83). "To develop and maintain buyers' trust and comfort," says a typical program, "you must attune yourself to their body language, their verbal responses, their unspoken requests . . . and modify your approach accordingly" (Wenschlag, 1987, book jacket).

There is a kernel of wisdom in this philosophy. No one likes a hidebound salesperson who natters on like a carnival barker, oblivious to questions and objections. At first glance the versatile, soft-sell approach seems not only practical, but even politically correct: a modern celebration of customer diversity. It's so hip. How can you go wrong?

But peek a little closer, and another image emerges. Soft-selling resembles another uniquely "now" phenomenon: Magic Eye® pictures filled with computer-generated 3-D images that appear to be just a random bunch of colored blobs until you squint your eyes just right. Then, if you are lucky, an eye-popping image of a Stealth bomber or a unicorn resolves itself out of the chaos. Like these high-tech visual illusions, soft-selling looks like an artful amalgam of deference and openness on the surface. But if you stare at it awhile, something else pops into stark relief: *ideological rigidity*.

The many ways soft-sell gurus try to align their gospel of inflexible flexibility with unyielding marketing agendas and rollout schedules can be quite revealing. Starry-eyed soft-sell converts may squint and strain and never catch a glimpse of the rigidity that lurks behind the gurus' colorful pitch. Yet, like those 3-D works of mall art, once decoded, it's difficult to ever see it again as merely an abstract jumble.

Lurking beneath the surface of soft-selling is a highly partisan philosophy. Ironically, the architects of the philosophy are not at all objective when it comes to issuing judgments on "traditional" sales philosophies (that is, any philosophy that is not in complete agreement with their own). The very definition of soft-selling describes an approach which is in direct opposition to all selling styles that came before it. That's what lends the soft-sell movement its revolutionary world view. The gurus portray themselves as not simply improving upon an existing system, but righting what they perceive as fundamentally wrong—namely, the sales profession's historical reliance on product-and-close-oriented selling.

"Nothing is more well-documented in business than the failure of the current approach to selling" (Hewitt-Gleeson, 1990, p. 4), flatly declares one text. Documented or not, the shortcomings of traditional selling are a major preoccupation among soft-sellers. They seem to devote as much energy to establishing traditional selling as the enemy as they do to promoting their own doctrines. A representative sampling of books devoted to soft-selling reveals that it is standard for authors to devote all or part of their opening comments to roundly *denouncing* non-soft-sell approaches. They warn that traditional product-advocating techniques are "manipulative," "unprofessional" and "pure old-fashioned nonsense." And they allow little room for discussion on the matter. "Actually," sneers one, "there is no such thing as 'soft-sell' and 'hard sell.' There is only smart-sell and stupid-sell, sell and no-sell" (Schneider, 1990, p. 104). Bang. Next case. Doesn't sound very consultative—or flexible—to us.

By contrast, soft-selling is typically portrayed as unconditionally virtuous, lacking only a papal blessing to secure it infallible status. In their impassioned determination to draw a line in the sand between their philosophy and traditional product-advocating techniques, the gurus are quite willing to suspend the law of rational consistency if necessary. In fact, many of their claims and assertions suggest a willingness to contradict their own supposedly inviolable tenets of soft-selling in the name of converting you to their beliefs.

Their rhetorical commitment to flexibility, for instance, is totally abandoned when *their* ideas are the product being pitched. Then they contradict themselves, lapsing into hard-sell insistence that you employ their proprietary low-pressure sales techniques—and that you do so exclusively. Is there no middle ground? They warn that even attempting to create a hybrid selling style, melding consultative and product-advocating techniques into an individualistic approach, is a "recipe for disaster" (Harle, 1990, p. 51). In order to avoid the cardinal sin of "behaving in a style that is mainly comfortable for himself" (Wenschlag, 1987, p. 167), it's best for the salesperson to do just what the soft-seller says to do.

Contrary to their myopic prohibitions against prepackaged, scripted sales patter, soft-sellers place a curious emphasis on doing things exactly their way. "Practice your questions constantly," orders one new sell author, helpfully adding that you should "expect to feel a bit uncomfortable at first" (Willingham, 1987, p. 35). Another proudly explains the results achieved by a group of salespeople using "a simple five-minute presentation" he designed for them that required "two solid hours of practice" every morning (Hewitt-Gleeson, 1990, p. 72). The use of "canned language" is a critical mistake of traditional sellers—unless, presumably, the can comes from the cupboard of soft-selling.

Upholding the principles of the soft-sell movement appears to be more important than the outcome of sales presentations. While assuring you that prospective clients will respond favorably to your use of soft-sell techniques, the gurus seem less than concerned about how clients act—as long as you are acting correctly (i.e., using their techniques). One shrugs dismissively, "If you have designed a proposition that truly is a win-win situation, but the customer cannot see it, then that is your customer's problem, not yours" (Hewitt-Gleeson, 1990, p. 56). Of course, the lost sale is your problem, your company's loss, and probably your competitor's gain. But, hey, it's no skin off the guru's nose—he already has your money.

Lurking within the gurus' shrill advocacy of soft-selling is a crusader's zeal which goes way beyond mere salesmanship—it's an epic quest. They strive to appeal to something deeper than your wallet or purse. Surprisingly, financial reward is seldom touted as the key benefit of soft-selling. Instead, in text after text a more urgent, spiritual message is preached: Our way of selling is not simply a different way, not even a superior way, but the *only right way* to *sell*.

The self-righteous high priests of soft-selling are convinced there is something inherently corrupt about product-advocating selling. That's why they don't allow unrestrained mixing of their ideas with common hard-sell techniques. Their objective is not to rehabilitate traditional sales approaches but to banish them altogether, leaving client-centered selling the unchallenged how-to-sell modality of the sales profession. The idea that the "consultative" approach is only one of many potentially productive ways to increase sales is anathema to soft-sellers. To suggest that some soft-sell techniques could be helpful for some salespeople, but not necessarily a one-size-fits-all sales-booster for the entire profession, is simply heresy.

Consequently, they twist the practical matter of adopting a selling style into a moral imperative. You must agree with the precepts of soft-selling *in toto*—or be reduced to the moral equivalent of primordial slime. "Ultimately it is our inherent personal characteristics that determine our success [with soft-selling]" (Harle, 1990, p. 1), opines one guru. With one neat maxim, adopting soft-selling not only becomes an incontestable measure of self-worth, but, with a little verbal sleight of hand, also places the burden of proof for the philosophy's effectiveness squarely on your shoulders.

We all want to be "good." Smarmy, virtue-preaching soft-sell hustlers know it, and play to this tendency in their pitches. They target the squirming Sunday school student in us all by tacitly assuring us that all "good" salespeople sell soft. "Learning relationship selling is not really learning something new," coos one commercial soft-sell program. "Instead it's adapting the way *you already behave* [italics added] to a new situation" (Johnston & Withers, 1992, p. 8).

Another best-selling text cuts directly to the supposed moral backbone of the soft-selling craze—the "I" word: "... the cause of success in selling is the integrity level of the salesperson. I can't sell above who I am—I can only sell consistent with the quality of person I am" (Willingham, 1987, p. 147). It's a sales training Catch 22: if you have to be taught how to soft-sell, you probably don't have the moral fiber to learn it.

Pitching Paradox

Not surprisingly, this logic works like a charm on salespeople and managers who are already beset by doubt, guilt and uncertainty. With the sweat-drenched fervor of a tent revivalist on a Texas summer night, soft-sell evangelists preach instant career salvation to sinners willing to admit the error of their ways—and fire and brimstone for those who won't. However, the zealous rhetoric used to pitch consultative selling as savior of the modern sales profession may be somewhat premature. As of this writing, soft-selling is not noticeably more providentially sanctioned or biblically grounded than any other sales approach. Absent that, soft-selling, like any claim awaiting judgment, must rest its case on other sources.

On that note, soft-selling has not been reticent to stake its claim to legitimacy on scientific evidence. However, after reviewing the evidence, there is a distinct lack of convincing support for the soft-sellers' lurid, evangelistic enthusiasm. You may have noticed, however, that the "ministers" of soft-sell are not inclined to wait for evidence or divine inspiration before broad-siding the market with hard-hitting rhetoric in the service of their soft-sell products. (Admittedly, that's probably an overgeneralization. However, some do come precariously close to claiming providential inspiration, if not direct participation.)

Nevertheless, selling style remains a matter of personal preference. It is not a moral litmus test. There's little credible evidence that plainly advocating your product, service and purpose—in other words, trying to *sell* something—is inseparably linked to mercenary hustling or moral anemia. Nor is there convincing evidence that so-called "client-centered" selling is as morally invincible or ethically watertight as soft-sell authorities claim.

It is certainly possible that under contrived laboratory conditions artificial distinctions between "hard" and "soft" selling might emerge in "what-if" experiments using university undergrads pretending to be salespeople and customers. Many studies of sales behaviors are completed in exactly that way. But salespeople required to complete actual sales in real world situations know that most selling situations are quite unique, generalizations are dangerous, and conditions cannot be easily reduced to a small set of inflexible assumptions necessary to conduct laboratory simulations—let alone properly study the complex interaction of all candidate variables present in the soft-sell philosophy.

Imagine you encounter a prospective buyer who prefers quick, strictly-business, product-centered interactions over touchy-feely consciousness-raising sessions. What do you do? According to one soft-selling rule, "It is much better to temporarily adjust your behavior to fit the buyer's style" (Wenschlag, 1987, p. 166). But, wait. If it's *always* "right" to adapt your style to the customer's whims, and always *"wrong"* not to be client-centered, how are you supposed to take a straight-on, product-pitching approach when it's what the client *wants* without violating the inviolable principles of soft-selling? The categorical claims of the soft-selling priesthood are wrong. There may in fact be instances when it's not always the best approach, which means there may even be other, better, alternatives in a given situation. If on the other hand, you can't and won't try to radically adjust your presentation to fit the customer's requirements, how can you continue to consider yourself truly client-centered? It's a puzzlement, and demonstrates how in the end, rigid soft-selling can become an exercise in behavioral self-contradiction.

Applied to sales techniques, ideological rigidity inevitably leads to this kind of logical tail chasing. Undoubtedly, some unprincipled salespeople use traditional product-centered selling as an invitation to behave unethically. But, which deserves condemnation: the method or the salespeople? To conclude, as many organizations pitching soft-selling do, that *all* product-advocating salespeople are more ethically suspect, shifty or morally underdeveloped because they use a product-advocating approach is logically bankrupt. The optimal resolution, of course, is probably to remain flexible when dealing with diverse personality types. Use what works. Just use it ethically. Ironically, that's the same solution soft-sellers would probably offer—if they were more objective and less invested in their own proprietary sales training content.

Smoke and Mirrors?

Look around. Can corporate mission statements, those regal bronze plaques that proclaim so-called "core values," reveal anything about an organization's attitude toward selling?

❑ **Kellogg Company is the world's leading processor of ready-to-eat cereal products. The company publishes a detailed mission statement which states: "Profitable growth is our primary purpose. We are committed to consistent, long-term growth in earnings and to superior returns for our shareholders. We want to be, and be recognized as, a growth company" (Abrahams, 1999, p. 269).**

❑ **In a similar vein, Federal Express Corporation, who provides global air express services, racked up 27.41 billion dollars in sales in 2004 and expects a 19% increase in 2005. Its' mission statement candidly underscores the importance of revenues. It does not try to bury or sidestep the importance of new business generation: "FDX will produce superior finan-**

cial returns for its shareholders by providing trans-
portation, high value-added logistics, and related
information services through focused operating
companies" (Abrahams, 1999, p. 183).

Some organizations, however, do not seem comfortable
using such candor. To them, indirection helps sweeten their
purpose and elevate their intent.

❑ Avon re-defines selling as "understanding" and
"satisfying." "Our vision," they say, is "to be the
company that best understands and satisfies the
product, service and self fulfillment of women-
globally" (Abrahams, 1999, p. 81).

❑ Harrah's (casinos) takes a more oblique position.
Their objective, it seems, is not financial. It's psychological. "Our Vision at Harrah's Entertainment,
Inc. is to offer exciting environments and to be
legendary at creating smiles, laughter and lasting
memories with every guest we entertain" (Abrahams, 1999, p. 223).

❑ Last, consider the rather convoluted purpose of
Tandy corporation. "Every day," they say, "we
give peace of mind to thousands of people who
need help from someone. We're here to solve their
problems and to connect them to the wonders of
modern technology. We are about people helping
people. When America needs answers, we're there
at every turn" (Abrahams, 1999, p. 412).

Contrary to the rigid rules of soft-selling, using product-advocating techniques is not the cardinal sin of sales. It is being intractable: stubbornly clinging to any sales philosophy, whether hard, soft or in-between, that is detrimental to long-term growth. Deciding which selling style is most appropriate for you in a given situation depends less on self-righteous notions of sales virtue than on your own ethical grounding, training and experiences in dynamic tension with real-world business demands.

Successful selling plainly requires achieving a complex but practical balance between product-advocating and client-oriented approaches. Yet the soft-sell sages' prohibitions against product-advocating methods unnecessarily restrict salespeople on hazy, moralistic grounds. It doesn't have to be that way. Used properly, product-advocating selling can be a powerful means of influencing people—one that is an accepted, even expected cornerstone of other professions. Politicians must campaign to get and keep power. Attorneys champion their clients' interests. They are expected to. Researchers defend their findings. They have to if they expect to secure additional funding necessary to continue their research. Members of the clergy are meant to. Can you imagine a priest, minister or rabbi addressing their congregation with "I'm not here to tell you how to live...I just want to be your friend?" Yet one prototypical soft-sell pitch ironically admonishes: "Don't begin selling...until... your attitude sincerely communicates 'I'm not here just to sell you something'" (Willingham, 1987, p. 71). That's like ordering people to be loveable before asking for a loan. But then, if you have to order them, they probably aren't.

Love, trust, caring, and sincerity are frail. That's what makes them so special. Fabricating them can be fatal to your credibility. Detecting the smallest sign of effort you are doing so, calls your sincerity into question. Put another way, any behavioral signals indicating that you need to be seen as caring will be taken as evidence you probably aren't. Dudley and Goodson (1999) have observed that the unethical self-promoter "Frequently uses words like "openness" and "trust" to deflect lack of integrity. Most people do not need to advertise their integrity. Unethical self-promoters do. They use reassuring words and phrases to draw attention to their *words* and away from their actions" (p. 15).

We ask, why shouldn't members of the sales profession proudly advocate the products and services they represent? They should. But they don't. The reasons may be complex, but one stands out. To us, soft-selling has been permitted to take hold on the basis of slick verbal gratuities, not probative evidence, to justify its dismissive, blanket disapproval of product-centered selling. In they end, what has been created is not the new era of professionalism they promise, but sales cultures ripe with confusion and needlessly bowed by humiliation.

Where in the World Can You Find An Honest Salesperson?

People exaggerate. Lots of them. Everywhere. Politicians have been known to exaggerate from time to time. Attorneys stretch things when they select what to include and how to argue their client's interest (Bok, 1978). Researchers in the hard sciences have even been found to tactically expand their conclusions beyond their data (LaFollette, 1992).

A human resources article about staffing reported that "Exaggerating on a resume is nothing new. By now most employers know what "proficient in Spanish" really means" (Inc. Magazine, 1997). A Wall Street Journal Report cited a study which claimed that "up to twenty-three percent of all job applications" contain exaggerated information (Mende, 2004).

Scholars and the popular media both seem to accept that all salespeople are prone to exaggerate the benefits of the products and services they sell (Lindgren, Byrne, & Petrinovich, 1968). However, according to some, that is changing (Wilson, 1997). Many commercial sales training organizations—mostly of the so-called "client-centered" persuasion—claim to be engineering a new generation of less manipulative, more "principle-centered" salespeople. As a result, there should be more ethical, productive salespeople who, it is reasoned, no longer need to exaggerate the features and benefits of the products they sell.

How much do salespeople actually exaggerate when given the chance? Has the emphasis on ethics-based sales training programs actually resulted in salespeople who don't exaggerate? Dudley (1997) has scientifically studied the topic since the 1980's.

According to a study comparing over 37,000 salespeople in eleven countries conducted by Bernstein, Dudley and Bryant (2003), exaggeration is still frequent and widespread. Generalizations are tenuous because the exact amount depends on which country you're studying. U.S. and U.K. salespeople were found to exaggerate more than salespeople in other countries.

Which group exaggerates least? According to Bernstein, Dudley and Bryant, salespeople in New Zealand and Singapore exaggerate significantly less than salespeople in other nations studied.

Despite the claims by originators of some commercial sales training programs, these data do not confirm a decrease in exaggeration rates. An earlier paper on the same subject by Dudley, Goodson, & Field (1997) suggests the problem may be overblown to begin with. Yes, some salespeople do exaggerate. But, they do not exaggerate as much or more than many other professional groups. Using the same exaggeration measures, Dudley & Goodson (1999) found that psychologists were also inclined to exaggerate. So were students. Advertisers posted predictably high exaggeration rates. However, one group discovered among the top tier of exaggerators was a surprise: consultants and motivational speakers.

Like any style of selling (or campaigning or litigating or preaching, for that matter), traditional product-advocating selling can be accomplished ethically or unethically, at your discretion. But it is *not* inherently wrong. It only becomes wrong when and if you choose to act dishonestly. If traditional, product-advocating selling becomes ethically suspect, it's because of what you do, not what it is. Despite the uncompromising claims of soft-sell gurus, dishonesty and "hustling" are not integral components of traditional selling. They never have been.

To Tell The Truth . . .

Professional persuaders, regardless of what they call themselves or how they choose to characterize what they do, tend to approach selling in different ways. Some salespeople may be more comfortable describing their persuasional efforts with rhetorical decoys such as "consultant," "advisor" or even more abstractly with currently fashionable terms like "influence," but all of these describe the same behavioral space. Each, for example, tries to shape attitudes and behaviors in some way, to some end, and can be practiced either truthfully or dishonestly. When people discuss dishonesty in sales and non-sales contexts, they usually refer to lying and and deception. Lying involves using words to purposefully misdirect. Deception involves the willful concealment of pertinent information (Thomas, 1985).

Somber toned speeches extolling the moral and practical reasons for salespeople to sell ethically are popular at sales conventions, and have been for many years. Some professional speakers have developed a lucrative cottage industry around the topic. One has a website featuring a checklist of "ethical behaviors" for salespeople—blatantly stolen from a copyrighted source!

Academic studies on lying and deception as practiced by some salespeople have been widely reported (Armstrong, 1992; Belizzi, 1995; Belizzi & Hite, 1989; Chonko & Hunt, 1985; Chonko & Loe, 2002; Chonko, Tanner & Weeks, 1996; Strout, 2001; Trevino & Youngblood, 1990). But many unnecessarily suffer from an internal weakness: a clear and unambiguous behavioral description of what telling the truth is supposed to mean. It may seem obvious, and probably should be. But it's not. Think about it. What exactly do we mean when we say salespeople should be truthful? Academic disciplines within philosophy and the social sciences struggle with that question every day. Definitions which vary in complexity compete in a Darwinian-like battle for the survival of the theoretically fittest. The truth may be out there as it relates to truth-telling but defining it is not going to be without risk. Nevertheless, for the purpose of this book, here are four behavioral "markers" you can use to think about what it means to be "truthful" especially as it relates to selling. The four markers we suggest are: Candor, Correspondence, Completion and Consistency.

❑ Candor: Forthright, unreserved honesty.

Joan, a salesperson for United Office Supply, has an uncanny ability to establish empathy with prospective buyers quickly. Prospective clients often consider her to be among their best friends. However, one of her clients says that after Joan closed a big sale with his company he never heard from her again. To this client, Joan is not very candid. She's a liar who uses friendship as a sales ploy.

❑ **Correspondence:** Claims can be verified against known or knowable external facts

Robert Ingerman, director of human resources for a large commercial real estate company, was considering a business proposal submitted by Rev. Dr. Reginald David Barfkon, a former clergyman turned management consultant. Dr. Barfkon was a natty dresser who's longing to appear urbane ordered the words he spoke and the clothes he wore. Laboriously emphasizing every syllable of words like "spiritual" (which he pronounced as "spit- it- u- all") Dr. Barfkon tried mightily to project a cosmopolitan presence, but was never very convincing. This was due in large part to his sensuous pursuits, chief among them, overeating. For some reason, Dr. Reginald David Barfkon insisted on being called "Dr. Bob," but no one quite knew why. Professionally, "Dr. Bob" had an oversized web presence, "The Dr. Bob Consulting Group, LLC" and an undersized organization (just him, working out of his home). Dr. Bob offers programs in values clarification, negotiation, goal setting, sales selection, conflict resolution, management selection, employee selection, organizational studies, sales recruiting, team building, and many other subjects. Dr. Bob is known by those closest to him as a "Commercial Christian." His signature style consists of the quivering, angry rhetoric he uses when he talks about the supreme importance of values, ethics, and principles in everyday business life. When Robert received the results of an independent check of Dr. Bob's background he was amazed but not shocked. It seems Dr. Bob's resume does not quite square with the facts: misrepresents his educational background, forgets to mention he was sacked by previous employers, habitually takes the work of others and claims it as his own, accused of theft by previous employers"…. and worse. When Robert tried to ask about the results during a phone call, Dr. Bob muttered a few un-clergy like expletives and hung up.

❑ **Completeness: Reveals *all* pertinent information; does not omit important details.**

When the Taylor family had unexpected bills pile up due to an illness in the family, they turned to one of the financial instruments their financial advisor had strongly suggested as a hedge against future emergencies. They called Howie, their advisor, who then explained that the instruments actually require several years before any benefit from their investment can be realized. Howie's final advice, given somewhat dismissively was: "Read the fine print."

❑ **Consistency: Unchanging over time, free from variation or contradiction; same today as yesterday.**

Lynn worked long hours and weekends selling enough new software systems to win the quarterly sales achievement award for best new producer. The prize consisted of a 10% commissions bonus and a week's vacation on the company's luxurious yacht. Lynn beat quota by 23% only to be told by Greg, her sales manager, that he had changed the rules and that she missed qualifying by 2%. Lynn didn't win. Greg lost his best new producer.

People need to be able to trust one another. Human interaction is based on that expectation, otherwise, why communicate at all? Trust helps to form our personal and professional relationships. Candor, correspondence, completeness and consistency are the behavioral building blocks of honesty. Trust is the mortar that holds it all together.

Honesty is more than a selling style.

"You don't have to love your customers to enjoy a productive business relationship. And they don't have to love you."

5

How Many Selling Styles?

"Hard-sell?" "Soft-Sell?" "New-Sell?" "Old-Sell?" "Over-easy" selling? These are all different stylistic formulations to selling. But, what is a selling "style," and how many really exist?

As the term is generically used in practice by sales managers and trainers, a selling "style" is equivalent to a trait-like cluster of thoughts, feelings and action tendencies that can be used to distinguish one individual's (or sales team's) sales-related behaviors from another. Selling styles are not traits. Traits are measurement-derived entities found in the study of personality, with very specific characteristics and uses. Chief among these are stability over time and across situations and circumstances. Selling styles may be related to traits, but they have not yet been shown to function at the trait level.

Selling styles can help management predict how a seller will act in certain sales situations and, therefore, can provide worthwhile guidance for selection, training and development purposes. In reality, applying "selling styles" in a training setting often leads to all kinds of psychological and philosophical meanderings by trainers, with the end result that almost immediately after learning "active learning skills" participants can still be found talking rather than listening, telling insensitive jokes, and chanting "Show me the money!" Selling style models, formulas and concepts are plentiful, and the number appears to be growing at an exponential rate, especially given the proliferation of web-based commercial offerings.

Merrill and Reid (1981) introduced the four communication or "social" styles they claim people fall into when interacting with one another. They are "analyticals," "drivers," "amiablcs" and "expressives." Their behavioral groupings look structurally similar to grid-type taxonomies developed earlier by management theorists, Blake and Mouton (1994), psychoanalyst, Carl Jung (1921/1971) (which evolved into the modern day Myers-Briggs Type Indicator (1998)), then back further through St. Augustine all the way to the model Galen proposed to the ancient Greeks. His blood "humors" model of Phlegmatic, Mercurial, Sanguine, and Melancholy may be ancient but its influence can still be seen alive and well in many of the selling style assessments used today

More recently, DelVecchio, Zemanek, McIntyre, and Claxton (2003) identified three selling or tactical approaches: customer-focused (need-based selling), competitive-focused (image-based, comparisons to the competiton), and product-focused (tactics aimed at informing or educating the buyer).

In The Five Paths To Persuasion, Miller and Williams (2004) identify five styles of decision makers: the Charismatics, Thinkers, Skeptics, Followers, and Controllers with proposed strategies on how to influence each. The model promoted by the Beilby organization's website in Australia portrays ten styles. Colorfully named, these include the Confident Communicator, the Culture Fitter, the Culture Breaker, the Enthusiast, the Business Winner and the Administrative Supporter. The Confident Communicator is described as the "classic sales person." The Culture Fitter adapts their approach to fit the "prevailing culture of the client's organization" while the Culture Breaker generally takes a radical stance, presenting ideas that are likely to be incongruent within the culture of the client's organization.

Another approach popularized by Wilson Learning in the 70's and 80's appears to be an adaptation of the Merrill Reid four sector grid. Another four-quadrant model advocated by Sales Training And Results, Inc. (n.d.) divides sales behaviors into Collaborative Sales, Technical Sales, Hard Sellers and Reluctant Sellers. In the web-based article, "Matching Your Selling Style with the Customer's Buying Style," motivational speaker Tony Alessandra (n.d.) offers yet another four-part grid. Alessandra's model shrinks style-oriented sales behaviors down to Director, Socializer, Relater and Thinker.

There are an incalculable number of other more-or-less popular models. Many are based on the Myers-Briggs Type Indicator (MBTI). Even more are probably attributable to DISC applications. The DISC questionnaire evolved from the formative work of William Marston, who also invented the lie detector in the 1920's. An attempt to exhaustively search the world wide web to obtain an estimate of the number of models was unsatisfactory as new ones spontaneously appear and disappear almost daily.

Science of Selling Styles

In the 1970s, research scientist George W. Dudley (1979) approached the topic of selling styles experimentally. Using two forms ("C" and "D") of the well-known Sixteen Personality Factor Questionnaire (16PF) developed by Raymond Cattell (1970), he computed an exploratory factor analysis of personality scores and functional selling behaviors for hundreds of salespeople. The result was one of the first scientifically based efforts to identify and classify selling behaviors into styles. To Dudley, a "style" was defined as a relatively stable statistical representation of natural consistencies in a salesperson's inclination to prospect, present and close which tends to resist change regardless of selling time, place, training provided or product sold.

Summary of the Six
Functional Selling-Style Profiles

Most salespeople show a statistically verifiable preference for one or two of the six different styles. Each has its own signature strengths and weaknesses. All of them have been shown to be effective in the right circumstances and under the right conditions.

Selling Style	Behavioral Emphasis	Underlying Assumptions
Service-Oriented Type (S-O-S)	Making commitments to support the product	People buy when they feel informed and safe about exactly what happens after the sale
Competition-Oriented Type (C-O-S)	Beating the competition, getting the order as quickly as possible	People buy from whomever sells them first; if I don't, someone else will
Image-Oriented Type (I-O-S)	Emphasizing the character, role and attributes of the sales-person rather than the product	Once people know who or what I represent, they will want to buy from me
Need-Oriented Type (N-O-S)	Asking open-ended questions to identify desires	If you align your product with people's uncovered needs, they will buy
Product-Oriented Type (P-O-S)	Reciting technical specifications	"Rational Man" - Once the product's function is outlined, reasonable people will buy.
Rapport-Oriented Type (R-O-S)	Using charm and endearment to establish and amplify warm, trusting relationships	People who love me will buy from me

TABLE 1. SIX SELLING-STYLE PROFILES

No single approach to identifying or quantifying selling styles is likely to be exhaustive or universally applicable. That includes our own studies. Multiple and complex differences in countries, cultures, organizations, products, markets, training biases, and in the makeup of salespeople themselves preclude the supremacy of any single model. The following section introduces some of the empirical research behind the points made in this book. It is largely based on three samples plus several country-specific samples. One small sample consisted of 49 salespeople acquired in 2005. A second study consists of 719 salespeople acquired during 2004. A third sample consisted of 3,359 salespeople also acquired during 2004. Using different samples helped us independently confirm our results.

Research

Which Style Is Most Popular?

A recent survey of 41,964 salespeople across several nations conducted by Dudley and Bryant (2004) found that 44% (over 18,000) chose need-oriented selling, followed by 31% competition-oriented, 15% image-oriented, 6% product-oriented and 2% rapport-oriented. Less that 1% selected service-oriented selling.

A sample of 211 salesmen and 241 saleswomen across industries in the U.S. (see Figure 1) confirms the popularity of need-oriented selling (72%), followed by rapport-oriented selling (58%) and image oriented selling (51%). It is not known if these results represent the natural preference of the salespeople sampled or biases which may have been introduced during training. Similar results from a separate sample of U.S. university students studying sales probably reflect systematic selling style biases emphasized in the curriculum.

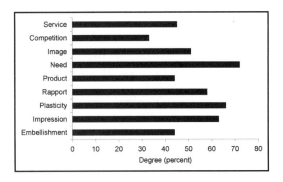

FIGURE 1. MOST POPULAR SELLING STYLE IN THE U.S.: 211 SALESMEN AND 241 SALESWOMEN.

Further, need and rapport-oriented selling, the two foun-
dational components of soft-selling, were the preferred mode
of selling in most but not all of the countries we studied. This
underscores the widespread proliferation of the soft-sell movement but does not necessarily endorse the effectiveness of the
model.

Gender Studies:

- Of the six selling styles, both saleswomen (74%)
  and salesmen (71%) say they practice need-oriented selling the most (Figure 2).

- Both salesmen (34%) and saleswomen (32%) say
  they practice competition-oriented selling least, but
  surprisingly, women prefer it slightly more than
  men. This suggests an imbalance between gathering information and resolving sales by closing.
  This can result in a *resolution vacuum* which can
  be easily exploited by competition-oriented sellers
  with less interest in identifying and matching client
  needs.

- Saleswomen (52%) tend to use Image-oriented
  selling slightly more than salesmen (50%).

- Saleswomen (59%) differ most from their male
  counterparts (56%) on rapport-oriented selling
  where they are significantly higher.

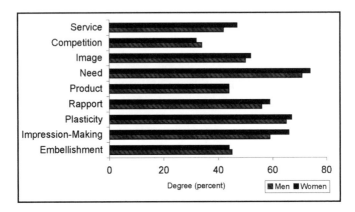

Figure 2. Gender and selling styles.

- Special scales used to detect faking found that saleswomen (66%) made a greater effort to spin a general over-positive impression of themselves than salesmen (59%), but there was little difference in their attempts to exaggerate (men=45%; women=44%).

- Saleswomen (67%) are slightly more open to considering alternative ways of selling than salesmen (65%).

- Service-oriented selling was among the lowest styles practiced by salesmen (42%), and saleswomen, though saleswomen were somewhat higher (47%). This suggests that American salespeople may be more interested in uncovering needs than assuring that those needs, once sold, are actually met.

Cultural Differences

Scholars such as Professor Earl Honeycutt (2003), at Elon University in North Carolina, have concentrated their studies on adjustments necessary to sell effectively in other countries and cultures. Comparing sales practices across three nations, we observed some of those differences at work (Figure 3).

- Image is important to US (51%) and salespeople in New Zealand (51%). It is substantially less important to Swedish salespeople (31%).

- Salespeople in all three nations say they practice need-oriented selling most, which further underscores, if not a genuine adoption of the method, the massive success of the new approach to selling.

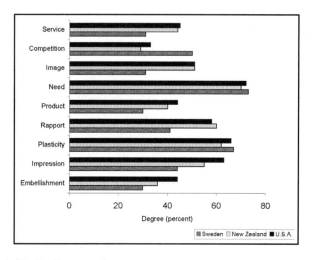

FIGURE 3. U.S.A., NEW ZEALAND AND SWEDEN: SELLING STYLE PREFERENCES COMPARED.

- Salespeople in Sweden practice product-oriented selling least (30%) but only slightly less than service-oriented selling (31%) and image-oriented selling (31%).

- Salespeople in Sweden (67%) tend to be slightly more open to new sales methods than salespeople studied in other countries (Figure 4).

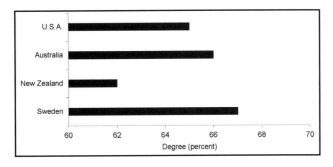

FIGURE 4. WILLINGNESS TO CONSIDER ALTERNATIVE APPROACHES TO SELLING.

Ethics and Honesty:

Retention and production of consultants at a well known international consulting firm had been satisfactory. Consultants there, as in most consulting firms today, had strict requirements for acquiring new business. A few years ago they were sold a commercial sales training package, which promised happier consultants who would remain with the company longer and would also produce more, faster. The program was ablaze with the buzzwords of new-sell. The organization, its culture and its consultants were consigned to the new way to sell. Bursting with new found integrity and a softer gentler bearing, they were no longer consultants reduced to common salespeople. Now they were in the business of identifying and fulfilling customer needs. They were advisors.

It started quickly. Production decayed with consultants posting annual decreases in sales. Then retention plummeted costing the company 60% of its consultants annually, along with its lofty repute as one of the most desirable places for high level consultants to work. Perhaps one of the most interesting and unexpected consequences of the philosophical shift was a sharp increase in mendacity scores on a psychological test. Mendacity, a form of deception, had been measured before and found to be within normal ranges for their consultants. It was measured again a few years later, following the introduction of the new values-based approach. By then, scores had skyrocketed to an average sten score of 9! (Sten scores range from 1 to 10, and fall along a bell-shaped curve.) An average sten score of 9 means the consultants as a group scored extremely high compared to scores obtained by other groups. Consultants no longer felt they could be honest. The company still has not recovered.

- A study of more than 3,000 salespeople (Figure 5) found that image-oriented sellers tend to exaggerate the most (55%) followed by competition-oriented (52%) and need-oriented selling (51%). Rapport-oriented sellers exaggerate significantly less (45%) followed by product-oriented sellers (47%).

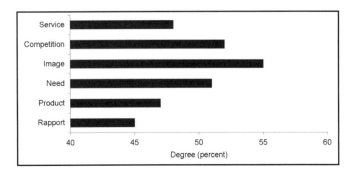

FIGURE 5. SELLING STYLE AND EXAGGERATION.

- Rapport-oriented sellers do not appear to be equal, however. Among rapport-oriented sellers, women (39%) are significantly less likely to exaggerate than men (51%) (Figure 6).

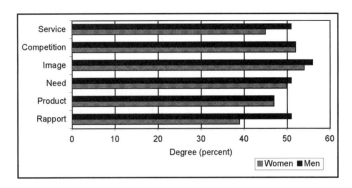

FIGURE 6. GENDER, SELLING STYLES AND EXAGGERATION.

Additional Findings:

- Rapport-oriented sellers tend to be more indecisive and hedge more when faced with making a commitment before they are emotionally ready (23%) than other styles. Service-oriented sellers tend to hedge the least (19%).

- Image-oriented (72%) and competition-oriented (72%) sellers are the most motivated to succeed in sales. Rapport-oriented (62%) and product-oriented (67%) sellers are the least.

- Image-oriented sellers (63%) are the most goal focused on their sales careers. Rapport-oriented sellers are the least (48%).

- Rapport-oriented salespeople (42%) are more likely to experience career limiting fear, conflict and hesitation associated with initiating contact with prospective buyers. Image (32%), service (35%) and product-oriented sellers (38%) are least likely.

- A study completed for a telecommunications company found some soft-selling incongruity. Trainers preferred and taught soft-selling. Senior management preferred and expected a more product-advocating approach.

- Preliminary data from a study we've just begun, of how salespeople like to be sold when they are buyers, shows that many rapport-oriented salespeople prefer a product-oriented sales approach.

Outcome studies fail to show the supremacy of any one style over the others. Though the verdict is still out on the effectiveness of soft-selling, studies show the unmistakable thumbprint of soft-selling on the sales mindscape.

"If you feel that tuning in to your customer's emotions gives you an edge over your competitors, certainly do so. But don't bet your next commission check on it."

6

Tricksters

What's the source of soft-sellers' passionate faith in the superiority of their methods? Moral conviction alone doesn't explain their uncompromising devotion to consultative methods, or the antipathy they express toward candid, product-advocating selling. The architects of soft-selling insist that the demands of a rapidly changing marketplace directly fueled the development of their techniques. That seems to be true—to a point. But there were other less obvious demands propelling the soft-sell revolution with equal force. The masters of the genre are somewhat less forthcoming about them (perhaps even unaware of them).

Soft-selling is actually an amalgam of several existing approaches to sales, none of which is particularly noteworthy or revelatory. We've already identified the origins of the movement in both Rogerian psychotherapy and in the time-honored ideals of customer service. Yet those borrowed concepts and techniques comprise only the skeletal structure and thick skin of soft-selling. It's the white-hot marketing of the philosophy that has vaulted it to prominence in the sales arena.

In fact, the movement's iconoclastic attitude toward traditional approaches may be the gurus' only original contribution to soft-selling. That's the angle that made the kinder, gentler sales philosophy a hot marketing commodity. As a result, it makes sense to examine closely the way soft-sellers themselves pitch their product.

To hear the gurus tell it, soft-selling represents a mission as much as a selling style. Their texts overflow with high-minded statements of purpose. According to these spokespeople, the goal of soft-selling is to get you to realize that "Every future client is first a human being, rather than a source of income" (Plotkin, 1995, p. 40), ". . . you must begin to adopt a philosophy that drives you to a higher, value driven, helping purpose" (Gitomer, 2004, p. 12), "develop and maintain buyers' trust and comfort" (Wenschlag, 1987, p. 166), and "start helping other people get what they want" (Johnson & Wilson, 1984, p. 21). Along the way, if you learn these lessons well, you should become a well-oiled selling machine, happier, more productive and more effective than you ever could be using old-fashioned conventional sales techniques.

So far, so good. As we have seen, it's no wonder soft-selling has enchanted so many sales-driven organizations. Its message is tailor-made for a profession chronically dogged by high turnover and low regard. Like a beacon slicing a path through the mists of the new world order, soft-selling directly speaks to the fears and insecurities of overworked, under-appreciated and often underpaid salespeople around the world.

Mixed Messages

Well, maybe not too directly. Even as soft-sell gurus seem to be transmitting all the right messages, they're simultaneously treating you to an alternate soundtrack of *subliminal* communication. There is a difference between what they say about selling and the messages their programs actually convey. Despite their stated goals, an attentive review of the soft-sell philosophy quickly reveals their passionate testimonials and adamant opposition to alternative sales approaches seem to be motivated by something other than concern for clients or the well-being of the sales profession. And, it's not just money; soft-sell marketeers are very upfront about their desire to sell you their wares, even proudly using themselves as examples of the financial success possible through soft-selling. Nonetheless, many soft-sellers are not cheerleaders for the common salesperson. For all their warm "up with people" pretensions, the friendly façade of soft-selling may actually be a bluff, covering up confused, conflicted, even antagonistic attitudes toward the sales profession as a whole. Some of these attitudes are communicated subtlety; some, blatantly.

"Even if you go to work in another's business or professional practice you may not be safe from selling," warns one guidebook on "relationship" selling (Johnston & Withers, 1992, p. 19). Their admonition turns out to be merely a preface to an entire primer on ways to muster a dignified, professional approach to selling, a task the authors clearly find distasteful but necessary. That kind of love-hate relationship with sales is not isolated or unusual. It permeates the soft-selling genre and oozes out with surprising frequency onto the pages of their books.

Sometimes the resulting advice is unintentionally hilarious. One example is provided by an author who compares selling with the art of seduction—right down to calling financially unstable prospects "sexually diseased partners" and equating sales presentations with "strip shows" (Sadgrove, 1994, p. 12)! No kidding. We can only surmise that this particular author must have been badly burned either in love or in sales—or both.

However, for salespeople who turn to soft-sell programs for help, the implications aren't very funny. When you invest your time, energy, and money in a sales program, you have the right to expect an atmosphere of authentic encouragement and support. Yet too often the soft-sell philosophy presents itself primarily as a way to make the best of an inherently bad situation (namely, your unfortunate choice of a sales career) instead of a way to proudly sharpen your skills in a legitimate profession. Worse, it requires you to implicitly acknowledge and internalize its negative presumptions about sales in order to gain full "benefit" from its teachings.

"To call oneself a 'salesman' is just like, in some circles, admitting to eating babies" (Hewitt-Gleeson, 1990, p. 198). We couldn't invent a quote that more graphically and succinctly sums up the toxic attitudes that assault salespeople every day. Unfortunately, we didn't have to; we found it in a book teaching soft-selling techniques. Furthermore, that statement is hardly an isolated example. Some of the speakers and consultants who promote soft-selling don't actually seem to like salespeople very much. Their pleas for more empathetic, client-centered selling appear rooted in the assumption that the negative stereotypes about sleazy, pushy, ethically-challenged salespeople are in fact true—not for the few, but for *most* members of the sales profession. Inconsistent with their assertion that soft-selling is the approach of choice for virtuous salespeople, many of the gurus, it turns out, don't seem to believe there are any virtuous salespeople.

Admittedly, it's a smart marketing strategy. If ultra-ethical soft-sellers believed that the majority of the 13.5 million sales professionals in the U.S. alone (U.S. Census Bureau, 2004) were already basically upright and trustworthy, their potential market would be severely restricted to the few bad apples who actually inhabit the selling barrel. By steadfastly maintaining a pessimistic view of the entire occupation then indoctrinating the profession in the same outlook, they can draw from a virtually unlimited pool of potential converts.

But as the basis for a purportedly affirming and empowering sales philosophy, the gurus' low opinion of salespeople is troubling. It can't help but encroach upon their teachings. Have you ever undertaken the tedious job of finding the bad bulb in a string of Christmas lights by unscrewing each one? If so, you can understand how one compromised component can taint an entire process. Likewise, because the primal energy of the soft-sell movement flows from the charismatic salesmanship of its gurus, their attitudes, both overt and covert, become an integral part of the information you absorb and use. By uncritically buying into their assumptions, you may be getting more "training" than you realize.

Soft-sellers may outwardly talk-up the sunny side of sales, but their methods seem to cloak a subtle assortment of darker impressions. "The new sales professional has to capture and maintain customers by taking a consultative approach," writes one soft-sell author (Carnegie, Crom, & Crom, 2003). "People don't like to be sold, but they love to buy" parrots both Larry Wilson (2001) and Jeffrey Gitomer (2004, p. 5). "Prospects and customers get the feeling that you're there not to sell them anything . . . but to help them select and enjoy the best value" adds another writer trying to talk-up the softer side of selling (Willingham, 1987, p. 34). A noble goal, to be sure. But why was selling excluded? Unmask the message within the message and you'll find yourself peering right at the unavoidable implication that prospective customers will respond to you *only* after you've convinced them you're not a (yuck!) salesperson. And this advice is coming from "experts" whose stated goal is to make you feel *better* about your sales career? Happy Halloween.

Statements like this are dangerous because their corrosive, double-edged messages are subtle and, therefore, likely to be overlooked and remain unchallenged. While they may appear to promote a higher order of selling, they may actually undermine your ability to feel genuine confidence in the vocation you have chosen, instilling a belief that there is something inherently undesirable or unacceptable about fully embracing the role of professional salesperson. If you're already conflicted about the moral legitimacy of your sales career (as millions of sellers may be), you don't need "affirmations" like this to confirm your worst fears.

But soft-sellers don't always blindside you with subtlety. In fact, their texts frequently mount *direct* attacks on you and your career. Although they often couch their diatribes in language that superficially appeals to your better nature, their words carry an unmistakable ring of contempt for the sales profession and those who make their living at it.

". . . [S]elling is basically simple. It is the salesmen who complicate it, and make it *difficult*" (Harle, 1990, p. 53), scoffs one author. Lest you miss his implication that salespeople who must grapple with the complexity of modern selling are simply too dense or morally compromised to succeed, he proceeds to rub it in:

> There are those who will tell you that 'Solution' or 'Consultative' selling doesn't work, that they tried it and were unsuccessful. Strangely, rarely are the critics from the top of the profession. The failure was not the philosophy, it was the inability of those salesmen to embrace it (Harle, 1990, p. 53).

Jeffrey Gittomer (2004) who immodestly bills himself as the author of nothing less than the *Sales Bible,* comments in one of his more recent books:

> Most salespeople think end of the month. But you have to begin thinking end of time. . . . If you think end of time, each time you are in a selling situation, the sales will always be long term, relationship driven, and referral oriented. And it has nothing to do with sales manipulation, or other seedy tactics. That has given real salespeople a bad rep . . . (p. 12).

Clarifying his position further, Gittomer, cautions with solemn arch-knowingness, "If you can't use these strategies to build your success, it is my highest recommendation that you get out of sales as fast as you can" (p. 12). Seedy? Manipulative? Salespeople who disagree with Gittomer may find *his* blanket indictment of their "seedy" strategies and manipulations to be somewhat seedy and manipulative. Most will simply find it untrue.

Do most salespeople have the luxury to think "end of time?" Many must think end of day, week, month, quarter, year. Like other professions, they have daily work requirements, deadlines to meet and sales objectives to reach. Many salespeople it turns out, like the authors of all those "how-to-sell" books they buy and read, have families to support, too.

Customer-Centered?

Granted, you need not conclude from this evidence alone that soft-sell promoters have less respect for salespeople than you thought. It's just as logical to conclude that in their zeal to reform shady and abusive sales practices, soft-sellers are genuine advocates for the consumer, who may be justified for sometimes coming down fast and hard on unprincipled sellers. Logical, that is, until you examine what soft-selling advocates have to say about *customers*. Then it becomes clear that whatever their feelings about salespeople, their loyalties don't necessarily lie with buyers, either.

As we've seen, soft-selling advocates a radical client-oriented approach: putting the needs, motivations and feelings of customers first, developing long-term, mutually rewarding relationships, and treating clients with respect and dignity. All this is as it should be. Showing consideration for your clients is ethical, effective, and just plain nice. Curiously, our parents didn't need gurus to recognize and codify this. They called it "common courtesy." Remember? We recommend it too, whether your approach to selling is soft, hard, or somewhere in between. But the fawning, excessive emphasis that soft-selling places only on the customer at the expense of you or your company smacks of overkill . . . that's not selling, it's a form of psychic groveling. Is the soft-sell industry trying to remind *themselves* that they can catch more flies with honey than with vinegar?

Perhaps they are. A close examination of the soft-sell movement reveals a disturbing undercurrent of disrespect for customers bubbling right beneath its advocacy of rapport-based, relationship-building techniques. Most rigid soft-sell programs pay lip service to the new breed of better informed, sophisticated buyers. But while they acknowledge the need for change in order to better serve these clients, they go overboard. Their pandering attitudes are as annoyingly servile as traditional approaches were annoyingly self-centered.

Who's to blame? Some gurus are quick to condemn customers as fickle, self-indulgent, spoiled children. "The idea is simply to treat customers the way they seem to want to be treated at the moment. Tomorrow they may want to be treated differently" (Schneider, 1990, p. 79). Others take a more cynical view of buyer/seller relationships that sounds suspiciously like a self-fulfilling prophecy: "You can't go wrong by assuming that people will always put up barriers when you approach them" (Willingham, 1987, p. 5). Soft-selling not only reads the customer's mind; it can even predict the future.

Possibly even more counterproductive are those gurus whose advice is blatantly hostile toward customers. Earlier we mentioned the author who considered it "the customer's problem" if he failed to recognize your selling skill. That writer seems to have some real issues with customers. He goes on to assert that "the salesperson assumes that his customers are stupid to the extent that they do not see the benefits and buy his product" (Hewitt-Gleeson, 1990, p. 56).

In his *Little Red Book of Selling,* Jeffrey Gitomer seems to agree with this philosophy:

> *I would rather walk out of a sales presentation from a prospect who says, 'Let's get right down to business.'...I don't win sales on price. I win sales on friendship. I give the 'price sales' to someone else. They're the biggest pain in the ass on the planet, and so are the people associated with them (p. 80).*

You don't have to love your customers to enjoy a productive business relationship. And they don't have to love you. A genuinely empathetic, friendly bond between you and your customers is preferable to a one-sided, adversarial transaction. But no relationship at all may be more beneficial than one based on a stereotypical view of your client that arises from weightless theories and is masked by a façade of smug good-will. A quote attributed to Andre Gide reads, "We cannot both be sincere and seem so." But according to the implicit objectives of some modern sales training programs, we can still do our best to fake it. Too often, however, that seems to be the soft-seller's model for sales success.

If you can't, don't, or won't prospect for new business, your personality, aptitude, interests, education, experience, training and good intentions are immaterial. So is your selling style.

7

Artful Dodgers

To a disconcerting degree, soft-selling is rooted in negative attitudes about buyers, sellers, and selling. Thus it is no surprise that the rise of soft-selling is intimately linked to increasing levels of conflict and discomfort salespeople (of all persuasions) associate with prospecting for new business. In 1979 research scientists Dudley and Goodson introduced an entirely new catalog of offending thoughts, feelings and behaviors salespeople use to cope with the pressures of new business generation. The psychological construct they originated is technically called Inhibited Social Contact Initiation Syndrome (ISCIS) (Baker, 1998). On the street it's called the "fear of self-promotion." Within the sales profession it's "sales call reluctance®."

Sales call reluctance artificially limits the career prospects of otherwise motivated, goal-directed salespeople by choking off new business development. Studies have repeatedly shown that it is more responsible for underperformance in sales than any other factor (Walsh, 2004).

Sales call reluctance is not a selling style. It's an *avoidance* style. Thirty years of ongoing research into this career-killer have convinced us of one fundamental rule of selling: If you can't, don't, or won't prospect for new business, your personality, aptitude, interests, education, experience, training and good intentions are immaterial. So is your selling style. There are plenty of client-centered non-producers and there are plenty of product-advocating non-producers. Style can influence sales success, but it is not a determinant. Studies show that most salespeople struggle with one or more forms of sales call reluctance (Dudley, Chonko, & Tanner, 2004) and that on average it costs sales organizations 15.3 new sales per month of tenure, per call reluctant salesperson (Dudley & Goodson, 1999). Where do these lost sales go? Probably to less hesitant competitors. Without an adequate number of people to sell *to*, your leading-edge sales pitch may as well be in some long dead ancient language, for all the good it will do you.

Many forward-thinking companies around the world have now recognized the costly consequences of sales call reluctance. They have implemented programs designed to immunize their sales forces against its effects, and have adopted diagnostic procedures to identify at risk neophytes and established salespeople before they experience a production shutdown.

But, soft-sellers collectively betray a rather startling naiveté when it comes to sales call reluctance. "We were astonished to learn that all but one of the people we interviewed had feelings of anxiety in sales calls" (Johnston & Withers, 1992, p. 7), admits one textbook—despite the well-documented fact that due to prospecting discomfort, 80 percent of all new salespeople fail to complete their first year in the profession

(Dudley & Goodson, 1999). True to form, those gurus who are aware of sales call reluctance nimbly blame it on the inherent seediness (as they see it) of traditional selling. Unrestrained by a complete absence of objective evidence, one soft-sell guru sees a causal relationship between the two. "Call-reluctance rises," he says, "as salespeople view the sales process as manipulative" (Willingham, 1987, p. 126). That's news. Hundreds of interviews with salespeople in many nations and tens of thousands of psychological assessments and a large body of scientific research have conclusively shown that sales call reluctance is not some moralistic protest against the nature of the sales process. It's the result of fear: physical, personal, career-paralyzing fear. Some of it comes from personality and temperament. Some comes from physical and biochemical influences. Some seems to run in families. Most is learned. None is traceable to any particular moral perspective.

Unlike other mortals, salespeople are expected to be perpetually upbeat and positive (although who decided that and why is another story). To exorcise bouts of doubt, conflict or apprehension, they are subjected to one pop-psych quick fix after another. When sales call reluctance strikes potential top producers, they take refuge in coping behaviors which they hope will sufficiently minimize their discomfort to allow them to deny, disguise, or deflect the real problem. Some hope to morph into trainers or consultants.

Many of the defense mechanisms they employ—from costly, inefficient, "alternative" forms of prospecting to shrill, emotion-laden defenses of selling—dovetail neatly with the off-the-shelf soft-sell techniques packaged for consumers. No wonder the gurus tend to turn a blind eye to call reluctance.

It's imperative that you not mindlessly follow their example, but try to maintain a respectful yet cautious psychological distance from their indoctrinations. We can't stress this enough. That's because "many forms of sales call reluctance are highly [toxic and extremely] contagious" (Dudley & Goodson, 1999, p. 22). Negative feelings about clientele-building can be acquired from popular stereotypes, corporate policies, upsetting past experiences, even passing comments by family members or friends. Some sales training programs, especially those of the soft-selling sort, can be a particularly potent source of contagion.

One ongoing longitudinal research project indicates an alarming statistical correspondence between the rise of soft-selling and increases in three major forms of sales call reluctance: Yielder, Hyper-Professionalism, and Role Rejection. Left untreated, each can have a devastating effect on production. Each can be easily acquired by uncritical acceptance of soft-sell attitudes.

Yielder Call Reluctance

Yielders can't say "no"—except to prospecting. They hesitate to prospect for new business due to fear of appearing rude, selfish, pushy or intrusive. So they chronically wait for the right time to contact prospective buyers. Not surprisingly, the right time rarely occurs, and potential sales dry up due to neglect. ("Close reluctance" is a first cousin to sales call reluctance and is commonly found in Yielders. Yielders can't seem to close sales once there. Asking for business, requesting a signature, and fixing a price to finalize the sale are all emotionally difficult. So they hesitate, draw back or simply escape the situation by leaving the sale unmade.)

To avoid conflict, Yielders are too willing to sacrifice their career interests to the real or imagined interests of others. They typically defend their (in)actions as client-centered politeness or consideration. But in sales there is a time for consideration and a time for considerate but assertive action. Many Yielders, out of their need to defer, wind up doing the exact opposite. By assuming that negative reactions will occur beforehand, they risk presumptively tuning out prospective customers, and turning over prospective sales to their competitors.

Statistically, Yielding is the most commonly occurring form of sales call reluctance. Research shows it's also one of the most costly. One study from several years ago found that automobile salespeople with high levels of Yielder call reluctance earned $3,236 less in commissions per quarter than colleagues who were not Yielders (Dudley & Goodson, 1993). Adjusted to reflect today's dollars, it becomes a $43,000 a year habit! Another study, this one from the financial services industry, found that Yielder scores increased steadily over a two-year period as the number of sales calls made took a corresponding nosedive (Dudley & Goodson, 1999).

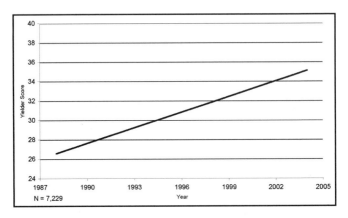

FIGURE 7. TREND FOR AVERAGE YIELDER PROFILE SCORES FROM THE CALL RELUCTANCE® SCALE.

The incidence of Yielder call reluctance in the United States has progressively grown over the last several years (Figure 7). Similar upswings have occurred in the United Kingdom, Australia, New Zealand, Singapore and other nations. Several of the countries where Yielder call reluctance is on the rise are those in which soft-selling has made corresponding inroads in the sales community. Many tenets of the philosophy coddle, ferment and even encourage, the fears of Yielders. Its emphasis on soft skills like empathy and rapport-building is predictably appealing to salespeople who are already uncomfortable with assertive client-building and closing techniques. Characteristic soft-sell beliefs, such as "Salesmen can literally listen their prospects into buying," (Harle, 1990, p. 30) tend to be music to the ears of Yielders who have emotional difficulty with the concept of talking people into anything. And soft-sell mandates against "manipulative" and "pushy" sales behaviors can quickly turn a benign mild case of Yielder call reluctance into a raging inferno of conflicted attitudes among sellers who need to learn to be a little *less* concerned about what prospective customers might think about them—not *more*.

Hyper-Professionalism Call Reluctance

Hyper-Pros can't say "I don't know" without grimacing. They have an insatiable longing for credibility and respect. To cope, they live in a "dress for success" dreamland where the *appearance of above average taste, accomplishment, refinement, sophistication and intelligence* becomes more important than the real thing. To act on that stage, they invest heavily (some would say obsessively) in image-enhancing clothes, accessories, cars, hobbies, university degrees, etc. Then they ostentatiously (but with style, of course) flaunt them at every opportunity, positioning themselves (with or without justification) as persons of elevated worth, if not status.

Hyper-Pros begin to believe their own "press." Longing to be seen as a person worth knowing, they start to become the character they portray. Unfortunately for their sales activity, Hyper-Pros typically convince themselves that doing the routine things that would actually bring them the high level of success they seek, and their image suggests they already have—things like prospecting for new business—is beneath someone of their character, repute and social refinement. As a result, Hyper-Pros become the best-looking underperformers on the block.

Hyper-Professionalism is most common in industries which routinely target up-market clients such as banks, brokerage houses and high end computer equipment, as well as in academic and professional environments where affected speech and exaggerated eccentricities seem to say "Notice me. I'm smarter than you are. You need to know me, I'm worth your respect." When using the voice and body to rigidly project an impressive appearance stops being instrumental to success and starts becoming an end in itself energy is needlessly wasted and opportunities are squandered. Hyper-Professionalism can be a costly psychological habit to maintain in any environment.

Figure 8 illustrates a study which reported that Hyper-Pro insurance salespeople earn about $24,000 less in commissions annually than colleagues who are less preoccupied with their professional image (Dudley & Goodson, 1993). In a study of the retail check-verification industry, account representatives with radioactive levels of Hyper-Pro were estimated to sacrifice 41.5 new accounts to competitors each year protecting their carefully crafted image (Dudley & Goodson, 1993).

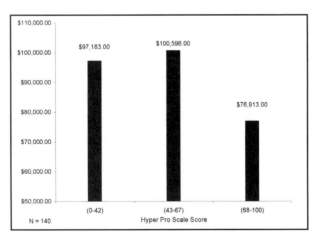

FIGURE 8. ANNUAL PRODUCTION OF HYPER-PROS: HIGH VS. LOW SCORES.

Like Yielder, Hyper-Pro call reluctance is on the rise in several countries where soft-selling has also achieved popularity. Are the two related? Consider the evidence.

Hyper-Pros fear humiliation. They surround themselves with accoutrements that will make them look competent, successful, and above all, professional to others. So they will feel professional. To them, professionalism is a feeling. It's no surprise they are attracted to the soft-selling candy stores that showcase ready-made integrity and professionalism waiting to be conferred upon consultative salespeople. At the same time, soft-selling demotes many "traditional" sales related activities such as consistent prospecting, which diehard Hyper-Pros consider demeaning. Hyper-Pros defend themselves by highlighting soft-selling's emphasis on seeking long-term relationships rather than "one-off" sales.

Incidentally, data indicate that the "advice" industry itself (motivational speakers, consultants, etc.) suffers from radically elevated levels of Hyper-Professionalism. This may help explain the consultant's prayer: "Lord use me in any way you wish–especially in an advisory capacity."

Sales Role Rejection Call Reluctance

Sales *Role Rejection* (another call reluctance type) is an insidious career-thumper that spreads an angry viral infection throughout sales forces, organizations and entire industries. Salespeople who have it don't know how to be genuinely proud of their accomplishments. They have an emotional career allergy. They are emotionally unable to buy into their sales career. Psychologically, they assign themselves and their sales career to the bottom of a self-damning career caste system.

Role Rejection strikes when salespeople, managers, trainers, even top executives uncritically internalize negative societal stereotypes about the sales profession. Once in sales, they believe on a nonconscious level that they need to be in another career. Intellectually they may actually like selling, and for a time even be highly productive. But underneath it all, despite their level of accomplishment, years of experience, products sold or training received, they are convinced they are a grave disappointment to someone—a father, mother, sibling, friend, professor or God Himself. Any satisfaction they do experience is often contrived and short-lived. Shackled by unresolved guilt and shame associated with their career choice, they are not free to enjoy and experience genuine pride in selling—although it may take years of silent agony for these feelings to seriously erode sales productivity, making each week, month, quarter or year emotionally more unbearable than the one before.

Despite the emotional turmoil it causes, Role Rejecters resort to a bewildering array of coping methods to keep their hopes and careers afloat. Chief among them is rigid over-positivism, that strained, peppy "Everything is great!" attitude that strikes others as glad-handing and insincere. You know, that mindset where there are no sunken ships, only submarines. In salespeople with Role Rejection call reluctance, rigid over-positivism is the primary form of denial.

Another popular trick is to adopt a "deflected identity"—a euphemistic designation that replaces the telltale offending word "salesperson" on business cards and in conversation—in the vain hope of fooling prospective clients into believing that you're not trying to sell them anything. "Financial Planner," "account manager," "business acquisition manager" and "territorial representative" are all popular deflected identities. Our favorite is "pre-need counselor"—a euphemism for individuals who sell burial plots, but deflected identities can range from "admission representative" to "purchase advisor." Applied indiscriminately and used improperly they all become symptomatic of sales role rejection.

Role Rejection is no laughing matter. It can destroy the careers of highly experienced, successful salespeople. On any given day, without warning and without a lot of fuss, some high producing salespeople simply hang up their sales brochures and turn their backs on profitable careers—forever. It's called the QWS (Quits While Succeeding) Syndrome (Dudley & Goodson, 1999), another telltale sign of sales career role rejection when it is detected too late. The emotional cost of battling unresolved feelings about new business acquisition on a daily basis finally overpowers the financial gains of putting on a happy face for customers, co-workers, family and friends. So they walk. Of all the debris attributed to call reluctance, QWS is probably the most tragic because it is the most preventable.

In many countries, the insurance industry remains a hotbed of sales Role Rejection. It's also rampant in multilevel marketing schemes, where participants (mostly novice sellers) are specifically cautioned not to promote themselves as salespeople for fear of alienating potential "friends" who might buy into the program. But it is also easily detected in many other sales cultures, particularly those which have only recently adopted a proactive approach to acquiring new business, such as banking.

Soft-selling is so irradiated with Role Rejecting attitudes they had to be totaled with a Geiger counter. After all, the entire philosophy is rooted in the assumption that most customers (with good reason, they imply) find salespeople obnoxious, manipulative, dishonest and lacking in integrity. Remember the "expert" who likened salespeople to confessed baby-eaters? It should come as no surprise that this same author recommends finding "a new name to replace the 'old sell' connotations attached to 'salesman'" (Hewitt-Gleeson, 1990, p. 167).

Sometimes call reluctance causes afflicted salespeople to cling to soft-sell techniques like a drowning swimmer clinging to a life preserver. However, at the other end of the spectrum are call reluctance types whose presence in a sales force will virtually guarantee the failure of consultative selling.

Over-Preparation Call Reluctance

One of those types is *Over-Preparation* (Dudley & Goodson, 1999). Over-Preparers are "techies" who feel most comfortable with voluminous information, detailed product specs and all the sales brochures they can get their hands on. Their selling behavior is characterized by a dire fear of being caught unprepared to answer a question—any question. In social interactions these data-dependent sellers tend to come off as somewhat distant, preoccupied, and formal. Does that mean they can't be effective sellers? Not at all. In some industries appropriate precision and attention to detail are assets. But Over-Preparation is not really about gathering information. It's about not appearing superficial. That's self-centered, not client-centered, and diminishes the likelihood that they will wholeheartedly embrace rapport or need-oriented selling, which puts customers in charge of the flow of information.

Over-Preparers: Closing by the Book

Both authors of [*The Psychology of Sales Call Reluctance*] are Over-Preparers. Trained in experimental design, personality theory, and psychological testing, our first-hand attempts to sell were colorful, but not profitable.

In preparing for his first sales opportunity, Dudley spent days practicing his only sales presentation, one he fashioned after attending a sales training workshop. About 90 minutes long, it featured facts, figures, charts, statistics, one unreliable joke, two feeble anecdotes, three marginally literate endorsement letters, and four obligatory "benefit" statements. Following all this, as instructed, was the close.

Among the things we aspired to sell with this strategy were specialized computer reports based on the highly regarded Sixteen Personality Factor Questionnaire (16PF) developed by R.B. Cattell (1970).

We arrived for one particular sales presentation exactly on time, as was our custom. Fully armed with a box of textbooks containing advanced technical support, several reports, various brochures, and an assortment of other inconvenient details, we were ready for the hunt. After a brief exchange of courtesies, Dudley catapulted right into his well-rehearsed presentation. Early on, there were subtle indications that the customer was ready to buy—including a few weakly veiled requests.

"What do I have to do to get started using some of these today? Who do I write the check out to?" the stout, honest-faced prospect said congenially, looking somewhat bemused.

Dudley seemed unaware. Instead of going for the early close, he plodded through more charts, more graphs, more statistics. The luminously smiling prospect courteously followed the presentation, but after a while his eyes seemed to glaze over and become vacant as if watching a motion picture from a great distance. Exactly 20 minutes into the presentation, a short break was scheduled. (Five-minute breaks were always scheduled 20 minutes into Dudley's presentations.)

"Didn't you hear him?" Goodson said sternly but discreetly, projecting only a polite ghost of a smile and speaking just loud enough for Dudley to hear. "He wants to place an order. Now!"

"That's impossible," Dudley said matter-of-factly, casually dismissing the issue with a know-it-all sidelong smile.

Eyebrows raised in disbelief, Goodson pressed further. "Why? Why is it *impossible*?" she asked, exaggerating each syllable of "impossible" for emphasis.

"Because we haven't gotten to the close yet!" Dudley snapped, growing more agitated.

Exasperated by Dudley's devotion to his neatly codified and exhaustively detailed presentation, Goodson approached the problem from another perspective, sarcasm. "Isn't it conceivable," she asked with the wiliness of an experienced lawyer cross-examining a witness, "that some people *could* be ready to buy before your sales presentation reaches the close? And isn't it possible," she implored, "that if we don't let this guy buy right now we might lose the sale?"

"Look!" Dudley grimaced, emotionally stiffening for a fight. "I spent 14 hours learning this presentation and this guy is *going* to hear it.

Excerpt from *The Psychology of Sales Call Reluctance* (Dudley & Goodson, 1999, p. 81-82).

Deflected Identities

Take a look at one of your business cards. Does it unashamedly say "salesperson" anywhere on it? Or, does it use a euphemism for the sales function such as "advisor" or "new business facilitator" or "product consultant?" All too often, sales-ambivalent organizations are eager to disguise what they consider the unpalatable mission of their sales force: to sell products and services. Once under the influence of soft-selling, they don't even allow their salespeople to be salespeople. Instead, to appear more "congruent," they pass off their sales force as an army of cosmic advisors.

Scientific studies (Dudley & Goodson, 1999) show that in the corporate environment, soft-sell attitudes and training programs find their most passionate adherents in sales managers, trainers, consultants and even senior executives who are themselves contaminated with conflicted attitudes about the legitimacy of the sales process. In company after company they listen to Zenlike mini-lectures promoting the new selling and then hastily implement soft-selling programs in a nervous attempt to mask their own unresolved emotional discomfort with the whole selling process—especially prospecting for new business—passing on their infected attitudes to their salespeople.

Here's one example of how these attitudes can be communicated from the top most tier of an organization:

IBM pays its sales force a commission. Digital Equipment Company does not. Digital's CEO, Kenneth Olson, believes commissions (the IBM approach) are unethical because the welfare of the client is more likely to be sacrificed to the monetary greed of the salesperson (Henderson, 1992, p. 95).

Do you think these comments influenced how selling was perceived in the company? Do you think they helped to instill pride and loyalty in Digital Equipment's salespeople? Digital Equipment Company no longer exists. Not unexpectedly, its much ballyhooed approach to selling was inflexibly consultative.

Ironically, the sales executives who perpetrate these client-centered approaches and soft-sell attitudes on their salespeople, still hold them *primarily responsible for increased sales*, even though they are no longer allowed to embrace the clear product-advocating elements of their jobs. The result in many of these companies has been predictable: flat sales, stagnant growth, downward-spiraling retention rates and confused salespeople. Are they supposed to advise or sell? Is their mission to acquire new friends or new clients?

What can you do to immunize yourself against toxic attitudes embedded in soft-selling as well as other kinds of training programs? How can you tell whether your own attitudes and feelings about sales are healthy? Take a tip from Ben Franklin: an investment in knowledge always pays the best interest. Keep reading.

Beneath the philosophy's veneer of credibility lies lots of anecdotal evidence, frequent appeals to emotion and to logic of the "Yes, that sounds right" variety, but scant empirical research to back up bold claims of effectiveness.

8

Proof and Provability

Aristotle, the father of logical thinking, reasoned that something cannot be and not be at the same time. One of the "cognitive awareness" questions we constructed for the CareerStyles Inventory asks you to agree or disagree with the statement "I can imagine a round square." Some people don't reflect carefully enough on the implications of their answer. If what they are thinking about is round, then it cannot at the same time be square, and intuition, willpower and a positive mental attitude don't change a thing. Intellectually, people understand this, but often act as if they don't.

The idea that something can be and not be at the same time is a powerful sales tool. For example, those coast-to-coast advertisements that used to be broadcast by "The Quiet Company" are, well, not exactly quiet. According to psychology professor Scott O. Lilienfeld (1996, p. 25), advertising campaigns like that work because of "the human mind's willingness to sacrifice critical thinking for wishful thinking."

In other words, it's not always necessary to provide objective proof; simply providing a desirable image can be equally persuasive. Consumer products from luxury cars to cosmetics trade on this principle. The hackneyed sales maxim "Sell the sizzle, not the steak" has now morphed into "Hey dude, why settle for mere sizzle when the nutritional composition of the meat will supercharge your libido and make you popular at parties!"

Today it's probably more fashionable to call this type of advertising "benefit selling," but the idea is almost as old as sales itself. To many adherents of the soft-sell philosophy, its promised by-products—more confidence, better rapport, more control over the sales process—are powerful benefits indeed. But does soft-selling really deliver on its promises?

Skimming through our research into the conceptual link between soft-selling and psychotherapy, we stumbled across a beguiling quote. Writing about various approaches to psychotherapy, R.M. Dawes (1994) said that assertions about the utility and validity of therapeutic techniques must answer to a commonsense demand: "show me" (p. 19). We think that's a legitimate demand to make of any sales training program, consultative or otherwise.

Ultimately, regardless of benefits claimed or implied, the strongest proof must be improved sales performance: increases in units sold and commissions earned. Not "job satisfaction," "supervisor ratings," "self esteem," or even tenure. It must be business closed and money earned. While there certainly are other compelling rewards to be had from finding the "right" selling style—including but not limited to those offered by soft-selling—their value is significantly diminished if they are not accompanied by a measurable and sustainable increase in productivity.

Most soft-sell gurus are understandably reticent to introduce objective research that presents a comprehensive warts-and-all view of their approach. The kind that science requires. So, in the interest of "facilitating a meaningful exchange of value," we present a sampling of some of the (admittedly scarce) formal studies that have been conducted on or about the topic of soft-selling.

Dominance: Once Sought, Now Sick

There's no question that the fundamental character of the sales profession in America has been altered by the influence of soft-selling. The very definition of what constitutes success has undergone a profound transformation. This fact is illustrated by a long-term longitudinal study of salespeople which looked at a personality trait that once was considered the hallmark of the "traditional" salesperson: personality dominance.

As measured by mainstream psychological instruments such as the Jackson Personality Inventory (Revised), (Jackson, 1994), NEO-FFI (Costa & McCrae, 1992) and Sixteen Personality Factor Questionnaire (16PF) (Cattell, 1970), dominance in its various forms embodies qualities like mastery, assertion, and competitiveness. Depending on the psychological test used and the statistical purity of the dominance measure, other behaviors are sometimes attached, such as jealousy, belligerence, and hostility. Years ago, top producing salespeople had dominant personalities.

It was expected. It was prized. It was sought after.

Prior to 1970, repeated analyses of dominance scores for salespeople in one large U.S. sales organization showed that high dominance was positively (and usually significantly) correlated with sales production, i.e., the more dominant you were, the more you were likely to sell. At the time, it was considered the essential personality ingredient by merchants pushing sales selection tests and organizations buying them. Dominance was the variable most frequently measured by personality tests for salespeople (Thoresen, Bradley, Bliese, & Thoresen, 2004). Social warmth was second (Vinchur, Schippmann, Switzer & Roth, 1998).

Variations on the dominance theme were humorous, if not bizarre. According to one sales training shaman of the time, dominance could be inferred from "eye contact" or wrist size. It also could be measured by observing skull structure, palmistry, handwriting, and by most of the grid-type personality scales of the time which, as described earlier, became the four-quadrant scales known and loved today.

For years many selection and training practitioners in sales organizations (who seemed destined to gravitate to hunch-based rating scales posing as tests rather than using properly trained psychologists and properly constructed tests) habitually searched for high dominant individuals to become salespeople. They sought them out and recruited them because their "go-getter" qualities promised the profitable new business they needed to nourish the bottom line.

But something happened. In the 1970s the longstanding statistical connection between dominance and production started to weaken—not incidentally around the same time soft-sell attitudes first began firing broadsides into the American corporate culture. Dominance began to lose some of its sure-fire edge as a predictor of high producing salespeople. Throughout the decade, the correlations between dominance and production relentlessly declined. Around 1980, it actually reached zero (Dudley & Goodson, 1980). Like mood rings, Est and typewriters, dominance seemed hopelessly out of fashion, doomed to obscurity.

But, believe it or not, dominance didn't bottom out there. In the 1980s, when increasing numbers of traditional selling cultures gave way to institutionalized soft-selling, dominance and sales production actually became *negatively* correlated. Dominant sales people tended to sell less than their more acquiescent colleagues.

Proponents of soft-selling could claim victory. The message was clear, they crowed. Old-fashioned hard-sell approaches no longer produced results. Thanks to the revolutionary influence of soft-selling, the market was responding. A new kind of salesperson had arrived on the scene, leaving hidebound traditional sellers in the dust. The data proved it, and data never lie. Dominance had become a personality deficit, which must be overcome with mega-doses of soft-sell curatives. It was out of sync with the times.

The truth was in the numbers. Or was it? Data can be annoyingly duplicitous and, in the wrong hands, maddeningly misleading. Knee-jerk reactions to data can lead to flat-out erroneous conclusions. We know. We've been victimized by flawed statistical reasoning a few times ourselves.

Did you know, for example, that conducting an orchestra makes you live longer? It's common sense. Longevity figures on famous conductors prove it (Abelson, 1995). For comparison purposes, the author of a study used the average life expectancy for U.S. males (68.5 years). Conductors enjoyed about five more years of life. Indeed, that's exactly what the author of the study concluded. The reason? Conducting is exercise. Conductors, therefore, get more exercise than most men, and that's why they live longer. Once published, the study attracted lots of media attention. The fitness link was reported by columnists like *New York Times* health reporter E. J. Brody who wrote, "It is believed that arm exercise plays a role in the longevity of conductors" (Brody, 1991). Common sense, right? Wrong.

There's more rubbish than revelation in the study. For starters, the calculation of average life expectancy for the non-conductor comparison group included infant deaths. But few infants conduct symphony orchestras, so infant mortality data should not have been included in the comparison. What about adolescents? Most don't like symphonic music, preferring head-banging rants of one tonality or another. So it is understandable that few can be found leading symphonies. Adolescent death rates also should have been removed from the general average. One critic suggested that a more representative cut-off age for inclusion in the comparison group would have been 32 years old, the average age of appointment to a first orchestral conducting position. The average age at death for U.S. males who reach 32 years old is . . . 72. Leading a rousing chorus of Wagner's *Ride of the Valkyries* may be good for the soul, but it doesn't necessarily lead to longer life.

Or take the recent study which indicated that cars equipped with anti-lock brake systems (ABS) are involved in more accidents than cars with conventional brakes. It initially appeared that ABS had failed in its primary mission to help you control your vehicle in the case of a sudden emergency stop. Naysayers declared the high cost of developing and distributing this technology to be a waste of money. It didn't work.

But further investigation suggested a more likely cause for the higher accident rate: force of habit. As it turns out, many drivers can't let go of the old driver's education rule against automatically slamming on the brakes. In ABS, firm pressure on the brake pedal triggers a computer to "ratchet pump" the brakes more efficiently than the human foot ever could. But because so many drivers with ABS still habitually try to pump the brakes themselves, the antilock mechanism is never engaged, effectively nullifying it as a safety feature. At the same time, these drivers, believing that ABS somehow made them invincible, began to drive too fast and follow too closely for road conditions. The real culprit was human error—not the failure of the technology.

Still, the examples just cited look great compared to some of the "scientific studies" used to prop up sales training programs. Most salespeople are familiar with the famous Yale University study that clearly linked goal clarity with personal achievement. The clearer your goals, the study found, the more you accomplish. It is one of the most frequently cited research projects found in self-help books, performance improvement programs, and goal-setting seminars. Not unexpectedly, it is often used by keynote speakers at sales conventions as "third party proof," of the effectiveness of goal setting programs, lending credibility to the off-the-shelf program they are selling. But like the vulnerable underbelly of soft-selling, there is a disturbing fact about this study. It's a fake. No such Yale University study exists (Tabak, 1997). Yet by repeating it often enough, the folks pitching goal setting made the study believable. But that doesn't make it real.

To discredit dominance, soft-sellers used specious logic to support their conclusions. They claimed that enlightened client-centered attitudes had supplanted old-fashioned straightforward selling as the way to customers' hearts. But a closer look at the data reveals another reason for the sagging fortunes of dominance as a predictor of sales success. True, soft-selling did play a role in its decline—but not the role the gurus claimed.

We've already seen that, in companies where it has put down roots, soft-selling is something of an 800-pound gorilla. It doesn't play well with other sales approaches. Its techniques are designed to replace traditional selling styles rather than supplement them. Companies which become immersed in soft-selling are likely to adopt the gurus' inflexible hard-line attitude and be intolerant of holdout salespeople with more traditional attributes, including dominance. Subsequently, environmental support for straightforward methods of prospecting, presenting and closing, dries up and goes away. Meanwhile, the selection process begins to favor salespeople who claim to espouse soft-sell attitudes. Less assertive, even wimpy, customer-focused applicants are welcomed into the fold, while candidates who score higher on dominance scales are politely eased out the door.

As a result, there has been a steady weeding-out of dominant salespeople in these companies. They either fail to get hired or are confronted with the challenge of selling within a culture that neither recognizes nor tolerates their selling style. However, dominance may have lost its place, but not its potency. To keep their careers intact, straightforward dominant salespeople have had to stifle their native ability to influence others in order to survive the soft-sell revolution. The most resourceful among them develop behavioral camouflage, which enables them to blend into their new, softer surroundings. They pretend. Those who can't suffer lower productivity, implacable production ceilings or, in some cases, total career burnout. The illusion that high dominance negatively affects sales production proceeds from this. Technically, it's the behavioral equivalent of the elemental "restriction of range" violation in statistics.

Now, (lest ardent pro-dominance activists gleefully co-opt this example for their own use) let us state emphatically that we don't mean to imply dominance is "good" or "better" than any other personality orientation—including empathy and other trademark soft-sell attributes. But it's certainly not any worse, either. The same factors that precipitated the declining influence of dominance help explain why it was correlated with success in the first place: corporate culture, selection and training methods, and level of support.

At the moment, soft-selling is favored by corporate decision makers controlling the purse—the golden child of the sales training industry. But twenty-five years ago, those same powers wholeheartedly threw their support behind personality dominance. Before that, it was sensitivity. Before that it was Positive Mental Attitude. Twenty-five years from now, the pendulum may have swung back again, or it may point to an entirely new success model. Such is the ebb and flow of fashion trends in clothing and in business.

Empathy Pains

The longitudinal study that revealed the current sad state of the personality variable dominance didn't explain what, if anything, has taken its place as a predictor of sales success. Could it be empathy?

Soft-sellers like to call empathy the cornerstone of their philosophy. Developing it, they say, is the key to the client-centered approach. "(F)eel what they feel . . . adjust to their emotional drumbeat" (Willingham, 1987, p. 22), gushes one guru. The more you're able to think like your customers and understand their needs, the better you'll be able to fill those needs. And that, goes the argument, leads to more sales. Like many of soft-sell's claims, on the surface it sounds very plausible. But is empathy really the heir apparent to dominance in the complex, changing hierarchy of success traits? Does developing empathy with customers actually increase sales?

Not according to a formal study published in the journal *Psychology & Marketing* (1992). Researchers examined the relationship between verifiable measures of empathy and sales production. They concluded, "Empathy is often described as a trait possessed by successful salespeople . . . (But) the results of the research contradict the assumption that empathy is positively related to sales performance" (Dawson, 1992, p. 297). In other words, this study found no empirical evidence that as you increase your empathy level, you increase your sales. Period.

The National Research Council (1988) also looked at the power of empathy to direct behavior. In this case, the empathic medium was neurolinguistic programming (NLP). A recently popular training "technology," NLP's rapport-building techniques have been embraced by many as a way to boost sales. Beyerstein (1990), however, expressed skepticism with studies claiming to support the effectiveness of NLP:

> *Though it claims neuroscience in its pedigree, NLP's outmoded view of the relationship between cognitive style and brain function ultimately boils down to crude analogies. NLP basks in effusive testimonials, but the National Research Council committee could unearth no hard evidence in its favor, or even a succinct statement of its underlying theory (p. 28).*

A more recent review (Onsman, 2005) takes an even more critical view.

> *There are various examples of management ideas lingering long past their use-by-date, but Neurolinguistic Programming (NLP) is possibly one of the more astounding success stories in the triumph of mumbo-jumbo over science... One key concept is "rapport," which involves using various techniques to communicate with others by*

matching their non-verbal behaviors, voice, tone, breath-
ing pattern and use of language. Once you have synchro-
nized all this, you're able to influence the interaction to
achieve your ends and presumably move in to close the
deal.... There is little evidence that NLP works and there
is overwhelming evidence that it does not (p. 16).

This doesn't mean that empathy is of no value. It never hurts to be a little more, rather than less, understanding. If you feel that tuning in to your customers' emotions gives you an edge over your competitors, certainly do so. But don't bet your next commission check on it. Despite the claims of soft-selling, empathy on *its own* is not sufficient to close more sales.

From the Horse's Mouth

In the final analysis, the most uncluttered method of determining whether soft-selling really works is simply to measure how much client-centered sellers produce compared to other salespeople. That's what we did. In 1994 we conducted a study to determine whether adopting soft-sell attitudes really translated into increased sales (Dudley & Goodson, 1994). We looked at 124 salespeople in a well-known direct marketing company. The group was divided into self-identified soft-sellers and non-soft-sellers. Annual sales volume was calculated for each.

The results are summarized in Figure 9. We indeed found a highly significant ($p<.0007$) difference in dollars of business sold between salespeople who espoused soft-sell attitudes and those with non-soft-sell orientations. But not in the direction the gurus claim. The soft-sellers averaged $35,210 in sales each, while non-soft-sellers produced an average of $46,076 each during the same measurement period, selling the same products, in the same markets—a difference of $10,866 in gross sales volume per salesperson.

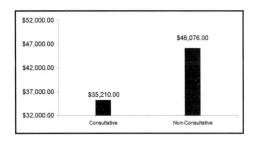

FIGURE 9. SALESPEOPLE OR PROFESSIONAL VISITORS?
THE IMPACT OF CONSULTATIVE SELLING ON SALES PRODUCTION.

There is no guarantee that these results would be duplicated in other sales settings. But the .0007 level of statistical significance achieved by this study indicates that the result is probably not a fluke or an accident. It represents a real income loss that is likely to be experienced by other soft-selling salespeople.

Other data sets provide some additional corroboration, but due to widespread differences in sales settings (such as the quality of recruiting and selection practices, sales training, and organization) it's difficult to form coherent conclusions. Salespeople in organizations undergoing mergers and acquisitions, for example, don't make very good research subjects.

There is enough evidence, however, for one conclusion: U.S. sales organizations using soft-sell training modalities should immediately begin doing their own objective outcome studies. Let the numbers speak for themselves. And non-U.S. companies, due to profound but often underestimated cultural differences, should have begun doing similar studies years ago—before mindlessly trying to graft U.S.-born soft-sell sales training programs onto the minds of their sales forces.

Competent research scholars at local universities are an excellent source for guidance on the proper way to design and run outcome studies so that the data you get provide answers to the research questions you ask. For the names of scholars in your area, contact organizations such as the American Psychological Association, the Society for Industrial and Organizational Psychology, Pi Sigma Epsilon, American Marketing Association or the professional governing body for psychological and/or business scholars in your country.

Soft-Sell Pseudo-Science

The conscripted granddaddy of soft-selling, psychologist Carl Rogers, once said, "I never learned anything from research. Most of my research has been to confirm what I already felt to be true" (quoted in Bergin & Strupp, 1972).

Call it the Soft-Seller's Credo. Beneath the philosophy's veneer of credibility lies lots of anecdotal evidence, frequent appeals to emotion and to logic of the "Yes, that sounds right" variety, but scant empirical research to back up bold claims of effectiveness.

Remember, the creative minds behind the philosophy are primarily salespeople, not scientists. Their chief marketing weapon is the logic of persuasion, which is quite different from the formal logic that underlies sound scientific research. Not that they don't wield that weapon convincingly. Take a look at these statements from two high priests of client-centered selling:

> *The truth is that when we fill [needs] for people, they'll unconsciously want to fill our needs (Willingham, 1987, p. 129).*

> *When a customer says, 'Just looking,' he means it. He's looking for someone who will take the time to find out what he needs and to sell it to him (Schneider, 1990, p. 114).*

The truth is out there, and these guys have cornered it. These fundamental statements of soft-selling *sound* right. They would be right in a perfect world. But the world is not perfect. Customers can be annoyingly difficult, unpredictable, and unfair. Attempts to control the motivations of other people are best left to carnival hypnotists and infomercial pitchmen. As a results-accountable salesperson, you should look beyond what the soft-selling apologists want you to believe and ask: "What have you really done for me lately?"

That can be a difficult question to answer. In reviewing soft-sell materials, we found very few studies clearly supporting the soft-sell approach that met conventional standards for scientific research.

*As pointed out by Bagozzi (1995), one of the most impor-
tant limits of relationship marketing literature is the
weak and often superficial specification of the construct.
More importantly, empirical investigations in the field
are very scarce (Kalwani and Narayandas, 1995). As a
consequence, knowledge of this phenomenon has been very
limited up to now, in spite of the recognition of the subject's importance in the academic and managerial world
(Guenzi, 2003, p. 708).*

Keillor, Parker, & Pettijohn (2000) comment that:

*Although most of the published sales literature which deals
with [customer-oriented selling] states that customer-oriented selling is mandatory for the professional salesperson of the 1990's, existing research does not empirically
address the critical issue of the impact of one's customer
orientation on that individual's performance" (p. 9).*

These researchers found a small, but significant relationship between a customer-oriented approach to
selling and average annual sales. Another group of
researchers found significant correlations between the
relationship selling behaviors of "interaction intensity"
and "mutual disclosure" with a self-reported rating of
performance (Boles, Brashear, Bellenger, & Barksdale,
2000). However, these researchers failed to account
for the effects of social desirability or exaggeration in
the measures they used. It is not uncommon for sales-

people to put a positive spin on things when asked to rate their own performance (Dunning, Meyerowitz, & Holzberg, 1989; Jaramillo, Carrillat, & Locander, 2003; Marshall, 1992).

Wagner, Klein, and Keith (2003) reported an important status differential effect. A relationship-oriented selling style was more effective for selling to middle managers (novice buyers) than to executive level managers (expert buyers) while DelVecchio, Zemanek, McIntyre, and Claxton (2003) concluded (after studying the differential effects of three different selling techniques: customer-focused, competition-focused and product-focused), that "these differences tend to be contingent on the buyer's position within that firm. When a buyer occupies a higher level of authority within his or her firm, [assertive] customer-focused approaches tend to garner higher reponsiveness ratings" (p. 39).

In support of utilizing a more adaptive selling approach, results of a study conducted by Porter, Wiener, and Frankwick (2003) state that "sales practitioners and researchers have recognized that 'one-size-fits-all' selling strategies may not be appropriate for all customers . . . and that an adaptive selling strategy will generally enhance performance outcomes" (p. 275). Researchers Park and Holloway (2003) found not only that adaptability was significantly related to sales performance, but also to job satisfaction and learning orientation (goal focus and desire to learn more about the sales profession).

In contrast to these scientifically grounded studies, we came across an expert who boasts that his new sell "system" increases sales by ten times. An impressive feat by any yardstick, but where's the proof? As it turned out, his claim was based entirely on one example in which the author himself was the only subject and three "experiments" with client companies (Hewitt-Gleeson, 1990), none of which reported using control groups, tests of statistical meaningfulness (significance), effect size, common indications of measurement variability or any of the usual hallmarks of serious experimental research. That doesn't mean his conclusion is categorically wrong. It just means the only verdict that can be justified is the Scottish verdict, "unproven" (Hall, 2003), and that his method was primarily poetic, not scientific.

We don't blame that author for sidestepping scientific conventions. Reporting genuine, supportable research results can make for difficult writing and, even worse, tedious reading. However, due to the nature of the lofty claims they make together with their insistence on appearing "scientific," it's absolutely essential to provide an acceptable body of evidence supporting the validity of their approach—which is unfortunate for many soft-sell gurus. Apparently, a convincing body of supportive evidence does not yet exist, and "scientific" is just another name they drop to affect greater credibility.

Most soft-sell gurus don't actually conduct objective research. Nevertheless, that does not prevent them from claiming to have "extensively studied" soft-selling and its benefits. To prove it, they pepper their speeches with convoluted scientific jargon and mysterious psychological buzzwords calculated to lend an aura of credibility. Even the most anecdotal, intuitively-based training program can be spruced up and made more market-ready by injecting it with convincing pseudo-scientific jargon. Words like "paradigm," "unconscious" and "psychological" crop up like soulful mantras, not to mention esoteric, bell-ringing phrases like "cognitive dissonance," "comfort-zone," "electro-chemical event" and "productive tension zone." One soft-sell author confidently refers to his approach as a "quantum leap, a totally new way of looking at the *physics* [italics added] of selling" (Hewitt-Gleeson, 1990, p. 9), as if such a field of study actually existed.

The bottom line? Be wary of what philosopher Susan Haack (1997) calls "philosophical hucksterism." Billboard language, anecdotal evidence and glowing testimonials have their place. They are language devices which soft sellers may use to persuade you to try out a new sales approach that may actually work for you. But these things alone are no substitute for rational or empirical proof. After all, the intent of the soft sellers is to get you to buy their programs, not to conduct scientific experiments. If you want hard evidence that soft-selling works you obviously don't get "it" as Werner Erhard used to say in his Est workshops. The buzzwords are the data. That people will actually buy and adopt sales programs based only on the *rhetoric* of proof, not proof itself, is the hard truth about the evidence behind the soft-sell revolution.

"…it's good old hard work and the promise of immediate (and high) fiscal reward that keeps [salespeople] on the road day in and day out."

9

Why Do Salespeople Sell?

Before conclusions are drawn about what salespeople need, more needs to be learned about what they really want. Much of what is "known" today about salespeople comes from the insights and lamentations of the same crowd that introduced the old subliminal message "technology" (based on another faked study), brain hemisphericity (right brain/left brain differences) and now, the new approach to selling.

Not too long ago, we conducted a multinational study entitled "What Motivates Salespeople?" which sampled over 40,000 salespeople in nine different countries. It was widely reported by the media worldwide. Formal results were presented to academics and practitioners (Dudley & Goodson, 2001; Tanner & Dudley, 2003). Results of earlier studies were published in the third edition of *The Psychology of Sales Call Reluctance* (Dudley & Goodson, 1999).

Although the study didn't set out directly to gauge soft-selling attitudes, it occurred to us that asking salespeople what they wanted out of their careers might be an additional indicator of how firmly entrenched soft-selling had become among rank-and-file members of the sales profession. If salespeople, under the influence of client-centered sales approaches, were truly becoming motivated by an extraordinary desire to solve problems and facilitate long-term relationships, it should be reflected in the results of a large study like this.

We weren't too surprised that the results of the survey failed to draw a definitive picture of the "typical" seller. "Salespeople" with a capital "S" are a fiction. They don't exist. Instead, like the practitioners of any profession, salespeople are a diverse group of individuals working in radically different settings. They go into sales for a number of reasons, sell in many different ways, and respond differently to various motivating stimuli—all of which you probably already know.

Survey results showed that there was no single motivator that swamped the others. Still, one response to our question did crop up more often than most. It probably annoyed soft-sell gurus whose programs were supposedly designed to appeal to salespeople who claim to altruistically focus on customers' needs. But it did make sense to us.

Show Me the Money?

What motivates salespeople in the U.S. (see Figure 10)? In a word: money. One in three said that what attracted them most to a sales career was "the opportunity to make a lot of money." Hard cold cash beat out creativity, service to others, even opportunities to break into management as an enticement to make selling their career.

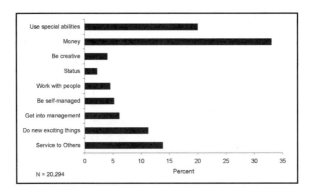

FIGURE 10. MOTIVATIONS OF AMERICAN SALES PROFESSIONALS.

What about other countries? Some of the other nations included Australia, Canada, New Zealand, Britain, Norway, Singapore and Sweden (see Figure 11). Thirty-six percent of the salespeople in Britain say they work primarily to earn substantial incomes. This compares to only 9% in Norway, 18% in Canada, 14% in Sweden, 17% in Singapore and 11% in New Zealand, where "lifestyle" considerations such as opportunities to use their abilities and freedom from routine are considered more important. In fact, "successful U.S. salespeople often shun advancement into management because they can usually make much more money in sales" (Dudley & Tanner, 2003; CBS MarketWatch, 2003). That further distinguishes U.S. salespeople from those of other nations, where sales is frequently viewed as a temporary step on the way to management. Citing Dudley and Tanner's study in Australia, Business Review Weekly (BRW) reported "[T]he biggest motivator for Australians, nominated by 28%, was the chance to use their sales abilities, and 22.5% said sales was most attractive for the freedom from routine it offered" (Lloyd, 2003, p. 60).

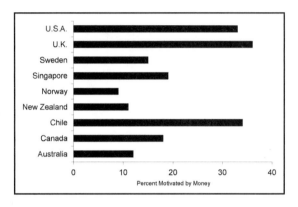

FIGURE 11. PERCENT WANTING TO EARN MORE MONEY (BY COUNTRY).

Dudley and Tanner (2003) found U.S. salespeople to be the most service-minded. Fourteen percent of the U.S. salespeople sampled said "being of service to others" is their primary motivation. Among the countries studied, only salespeople in New Zealand (11.5%) approached that level of service-orientation. Australian salespeople were lower (8.6%) but not among the lowest. Salespeople in Norway (1.6%), Sweden (3.2%), and the U.K. (3.7%) were lower. Professor Clive Fletcher (personal communication, October 11, 2003), emeritus Professor of Psychology, University of London and Managing Director of Personnel Assessment Ltd., says Dudley and Tanner's results may be "another indicator that over time it has become more socially acceptable in the U.K. to admit that one is interested in making money." Fletcher points out, however, that U.K. salespeople "may have a way to go on the service motivation front."

If you've been successfully indoctrinated in soft-selling, you may experience some cognitive dissonance when reading the results of this study. According to the architects of the philosophy, soft-selling is responsible for the creation of a new breed of seller, one who is principally motivated by a sincere desire to create value for customers—one who is chiefly concerned with a harmonious sales process, not with the crass matter of earning commissions. Being motivated by money is an outdated hard-sell attitude, a zit endangering the modern sales complexion.

Yet a strong plurality of salespeople say they chose sales primarily to make a lot of money. Could there be heretics in the congregation? According to orthodox soft-selling theologians, these salespeople are not only wrong, they're selfish, overbearing Philistines. Although the proportion endorsing money as the primary reason for being in sales varied by country (Norway was at the bottom), the salespeople we surveyed said that motivators like "serving others" finished well back in the ranks compared to the prospect of earning unlimited financial rewards.

Sales Training Across Cultures?

Knowing what makes salespeople tick is critical for finding and keeping top producers. According to Jeff Tanner (Yahoo! Finance, 2003; Weitz, Castleberry, & Tanner, 1992), co-author of a leading university level textbook on selling, "the implications are serious and far-reaching, especially when it comes to multinational sales management practices. American sales management and training procedures usually reflect our values and perceptions and may not be optimal, or even suitable, for use in other countries. Sales managers in those countries should probably evaluate home-grown sales management resources first, then seek outside resources only as needed." Professor Earl Honeycutt (2003), co-author of *Sales Management: a Global Perspective*, concurs and adds that "Global firms must insure training content and sales methods match local taste and culture . . . 'soft-skills,' such as supervisory or communication skills, should be adapted to match local practices; however, more technical skills can be standardized" (p. 129).

As Aristotle implied, you can't have it both ways. Either salespeople are doing a quick two-step claiming to embrace high minded soft-selling virtues while still chanting "show me the money!," or soft-sell gurus themselves are ducking the contradiction by claiming that sellers are most fulfilled by ephemera such as service and rapport-building—when in fact it's good old hard work and the promise of immediate (and high) fiscal reward that keeps them on the road day in and day out.

"Stop and think. Have you ever seen the leading lights of the soft-sell industry pitching their soft-sell training programs by actually using soft-sell techniques?"

10

Embarrassed to Be Me?

Your sales manager has just adopted a new soft-sell agenda for the entire sales force. You are expected to use a euphemistic identity and touchy-feely approaches to handling clients. Or perhaps you've simply decided to give soft-selling a try yourself. In any event, you now have two options for maintaining productivity and preserving your sanity: either completely jettison the "traditional" selling notions you have relied on in the past, or somehow try to integrate two radically different philosophies into your selling strategy. But how?

The sales profession is already complex, fast-paced and demanding. Forging a successful career is a never-ending challenge no matter how you go about it. It only complicates matters that management continues to demand old-fashioned sales results, even while touting a new softer, advising, not-selling culture. Hardworking, well-intentioned salespeople, forced to splice together a workable selling strategy from conflicting objectives, have had to be extraordinarily creative just to survive. Many don't.

Those that do learn to parrot all the politically correct soft-sell buzzwords. But at the same time, many are cold realists at heart. They have to be. They realize that to continue to earn a decent income they have to do more than just make friends with potential buyers; they have to get things sold. So, like punch-drunk boxers, they wobble, bob and weave, mouthing idealistic soft-sell jargon to satisfy management, but reverting to product-advocating methods to close sales. Many haven't fully committed to either approach, and at the same time they're not entirely comfortable with the compromise they've reached either. Nevertheless, they've bought (or been sold) the belief that the approaches represent parallel lines, never crossing, never bending, always to remain separate and repellent.

It's a pity. In their attempts to introduce their salespeople to a brave new world of selling, many sales organizations have forced them to become old-fashioned hypocrites instead.

But take heart. It doesn't have to be that way. Another ending can be written. It's your career. Let self-worth (or if that is not sufficient, self-preservation) be your guide. Approach all newfangled selling methods with a respectful combination of hopeful enthusiasm, open-mindedness and healthy skepticism. Even if your sales management is totally committed to overhauling the selling process, remember that you're the one who has to close sales. So be prudent. Here's how.

The first step is evaluation. Before you capitulate to soft-selling, or try any other new sales approach for that matter, perform your own feasibility study first.

Use these criteria as a starting point:

1. Is the new approach *effective*? Where's the proof?

2. Is it *appropriate* for my market, product line, skill level, selling environment?

3. Does it *feel "right"* to me? Will it enhance or diminish my career? Would I recommend it to members of my own family if they were in sales?

If the answer to all these questions is "yes," give yourself permission to provisionally try out the new approach, whether it's relationship selling, some new prospecting technique, another gee-whiz "body language" book, or even one of those tedious volumes claiming to teach you how to hypnotize your clients into buying. But if a selling modality falls short on one or more criteria—if it fails to prove its effectiveness, appropriateness or "rightness" to your satisfaction—immediately build a protective psychological perimeter around your wallet and cautiously back away. Further study is in order. Can you speak with, or read about, other salespeople who have found success with the new method? Do you understand why your manager, trainer, etc. recommended it? Have you had sufficient opportunity to evaluate it for yourself? Before you reject a sales technique outright, however, consider other options. Even if a given approach fails your feasibility study, it may still be possible take advantage of some of its strengths.

You can try to *accommodate* it: try to change something about your current situation that will make the new approach a better fit. For example, if you've rejected a telephone prospecting technique because you typically don't do telephone prospecting for new business, commit to making, say, just five calls a week for a month to see if it really does increase your business.

You can *adapt* the approach to what you're already doing, either by altering it or by adopting only those aspects which are compatible with your current practices. For instance, many salespeople rely heavily on buyers' body language signals to gauge attitudes. Obviously, this approach won't work if you sell primarily by phone. But it might be worthwhile to learn about barely audible vocal tremors (voice stress indicators) to help you better track your prospect's receptivity.

If these options fail to produce satisfactory results, you can simply *avoid* the new approach altogether. You carefully considered it, possibly even gave it a trial run, and it just didn't pass the test. It's time to move on to more productive sales activities. Some soft-sellers will try to directly or indirectly belittle you if you find their approach lacking. It becomes your fault, a failure of character or intelligence or both. Don't let yourself be scammed and taken on that guilt trip. The only thing that rejecting soft-selling (or any other sales approach) says about you is that you think for yourself.

Finally, you could *abdicate* responsibility for your own career and become so overwhelmed by the daunting task of crafting a totally dazzling selling style that, like the quest for the career, car or lover, you simply throw up your hands and allow yourself to be swept along by prevailing currents to wherever they may lead you. Using this strategy, you could be lucky and drift into prosperity and fulfillment. However, it's more likely that you'll eventually find yourself unceremoniously washed up.

Whatever you do, don't fall victim to the marketing ploy that soft-selling is wholly incompatible with other sales approaches. It's not. Despite high-voltage warnings to the contrary, many a la carte elements of the soft-sell philosophy may fit well with your current selling style. If that's so, you owe it to your career to give them a fair trial. For example, asking open-ended questions—an important soft-sell technique—can be a helpful way to reduce threat, put customers at ease and get them to describe what they expect from you and your product or service. But don't stop there. Once you've learned about their needs and aligned them with your product, *ask for the order*. Don't wait for them "to see the light" and close the sale for you. That's *your* job. That's what professional salespeople do. That's what they are expected to do.

Soft-sell pitchmen and women have purposely encouraged an antagonistic relationship between the two selling styles, client-centered and product-centered. Their simplistic carica-ture of the two has been effective in part because they have successfully invoked an artificial soft-sell/hard-sell dichotomy and then presented it as if it were true. Cognitive psycholo-gists call this process "dichotomous thinking," all-or-nothing portrayals used to distort information and influence poor deci-sion making (Shapiro, 1995). Soft-selling is positioned as the polar opposite of traditional selling: honest instead of dishonest, consultative instead of manipulative, chummy instead of adver-sarial. The virtues they attribute to soft-selling are admirable; the ones conferred on others, are not. But is this a fair portrayal? Yes, if you also believe all European cars are reliable and efficient, but all American cars are gas guzzlers and prone to breaking down.

In reality, market economies have a Machiavellian tendency to weed out ineffective sellers, regardless of style. "Good" selling is simply that which produces profitable long-term growth. But "good" selling can quickly turn to "bad" selling when it becomes so self-righteous and parochial that it can no longer recognize and respond to changing conditions. Ask the founder of the late Digital Equipment Corporation.

We don't have an axe to grind against soft-selling. There's no personal vendetta. Its abstract, arbitrary principles are no more or less guilty of propagating misinformation about the nature of sales than the abstract, arbitrary rules of any sales training "technology" based mostly on anecdotes and testimonials. But unlike competing models it has a major structural flaw. It mistakenly presumes that ethical behavior and sales productivity come from your choice of a selling style (namely theirs)–when in truth they emanate from you.

In one sense we agree with the high priests of soft-selling that there are two opposing philosophies of selling. But to us, it's not the new fuzzy approach to selling versus the old, conventional approach. One of the two radically differing stances is overt productive, above-board selling. The other is covert and leads to conflict, frustration, and hesitation. The distinction isn't between "hard" and "soft" selling. And it isn't between "product-centered" and "client-centered" sales, either. The difference between success and failure in sales boils down to an elemental choice you make every time you initiate contact with a current or prospective customer. Will my selling efforts *be intentional* or *compensatory*?

Intentional Selling

Unlike the esoteric recipes for soft-selling, intentional and compensatory selling are defined by *your* goals and/or the goals of your organization. "Intention" is a technical designation, used in German psychologist Julius Kuhl's (Kuhl & Beckman, 1994) theory of action control. Action control theory is a well-researched attempt to better understand why some people are able to take action consistent with their goals while others get bogged down by all sorts of convoluted behavior-inhibiting thoughts and feelings.

The term "intention," as Kuhl uses it, builds on other goal-related notions such as *importance, urgency and competence.* "[U]nlike many theorists, we do not use the term intention for any long term goal or wish," Kuhl writes. "Rather, we restrict our use of the term to those goals to which an individual is currently committed" (Kuhl, 1994, p. 101).

An in-depth explanation of Kuhl's theory is well beyond the scope of this book. But his work is important to our discussion for two reasons. First, it parallels the theoretical model of impaired prospecting (sales call reluctance) which was outlined earlier and shown to be one logical outcome of rigid soft-selling. Second, it more closely matches and expands upon what we mean by intentional selling than any other scientifically based model.

Intentionality is a concept that helps "bridge the gap between choice and action" (Kuhl and Beckmann, p. 9). Simply put, your selling is intentional if you acknowledge that your primary goal is to close sales, earn commissions and responsibly get your product into the hands of the people who need it. Inevitably you will try to accomplish that goal in a way that is consistent with your values, whatever they are. But "values" is an extraordinarily complicated buzzword tossed airily about by the soft-sell crowd, which seems to think it's merely another synonym for personal beliefs, principles, or morals (Adler, 1997). It's not. It's much more complex than that, and for starters requires complex "philosophical assumptions of consciousness, the self, and free will" (Shapiro, Schwartz, & Astin, 1996, p. 1223).

Intentional selling, like purposeful driving or deliberate career selection, is about choices you can make. It is selling without apology. It's sales with an attitude. It's disclosing your purpose with dignity. And it is no more or less preoccupied with trying to meet everyone else's criteria for acceptable behavior than responsible people in any career should be.

In any event, intentionality is not measured by the moral acceptablility of your techniques. As you can imagine, that requires an entirely different yardstick. It is measured instead by the forthrightness of your actions. And if you are in sales, that's a choice you can make and do make all the time. You can choose a non-confrontational, service-oriented approach to persuade people to buy from you. Or you can try to nudge your customers along with higher pressure. Either way, from a bottom line standpoint, the goal remains the same.

On the other hand, if your *primary* goal in selling is to avoid negative reactions, bolster flagging confidence in your sales career or hide the persuasive nature of your job from yourself and your customers, then your selling—regardless of style—is *compensatory*. It is counter-intentional. When you begin to feel that fat commission checks no longer obliterate the emotional pain associated with having to face customers, friends, and family members who may perceive your sales career as somehow sleazy, inferior or disappointing, you run the risk of activating unproductive coping mechanisms to compensate for the underlying discomfort and loss that constantly shadow your selling efforts.

But unlike the simplistic stereotypes promoted by soft-sellers, the behavioral maneuvers of salespeople caught in compensatory selling modes go beyond hard/soft distinctions. Fast-talking hustlers with super-positive, damn-the-torpedoes let's-make-a-deal approaches are practicing compensatory selling. But so are you when you try to soft-sell your customers in a way they find equally annoying, suspicious, frustrating and rigid. Try responding to a customer's rapid-fire request for bottom line information by launching into a discussion of their needs as interpreted by you. Or refuse to close a sale until you've "validated" yourself to a client who just wants to get the purchase completed. Any time a salesperson thinks a sale hinges on good vibrations, you can be sure compensatory selling has taken over.

Intentional sellers focus their energy on doing the things—prospecting, presenting, closing, serving—that will move them responsibly, competently and consistently closer to their goals. Although they are not immune to normal bouts of self-doubt and excuse making, they recognize those impulses for what they are—unproductive—and don't allow them to impede or alter their sales activities. Compensatory sellers, on the other hand, divert all their energy into coping with unresolved doubts about their career, with other people's perceptions, and with trying to distance themselves from negative attitudes about the sales process which they cannot control.

Soft-selling is not innately compensatory in nature. And product-advocating selling is not always intentional. But many soft-sell techniques *are* thinly disguised coping mechanisms, designed not to increase the *buyer's* comfort (as claimed) but to soothe the *salesperson's* discomfort with selling. They're compensatory because they seek to redefine the nature of your work in such a way as to make you feel you're doing something better or nobler than merely "pushing product."

It's all in the intentions. For instance, there's absolutely nothing wrong with calling yourself an "advisor" if you like the sound of the title. But if you feel you must remove "salesperson" from your business card because you think the word itself turns people off or makes them act differently toward you, stop and think. Is your feeling based on actual experiences with customers, or is it based on fears of *what might happen* if a customer took offense at your job title? And regardless of what others may or may not think, how many sales calls could you have made while you were busy searching for a less "offensive" title and ordering new business cards from the printer?

Likewise, if you find it easier to close sales by first establishing rapport with your customers, by all means do so. In some cultures, small talk and questions about the client's personal life are expected to precede the development of a business relationship. But don't fall into the trap of thinking that a warm relationship *must* exist prior to closing a sale. The moment you do that, the goal of your sales presentation shifts from new business generation to rapport-building. Your approach ceases to be intentional.

Professional "sales" encompasses a far-ranging variety of activities, many of which soft-selling seems to have ignored in formulating its philosophy. Late-night television commercials pitching Ginsu knives to bleary-eyed consumers are "selling" just as surely as complex global business-to-business transactions are "selling." The housewife trying to persuade a young child to try a new food for the first time is selling, as are the professors trying to persuade sociology students to stay awake and the scientist writing grants to secure research funding.

While many of soft-selling's techniques seem preoccupied with mega-sized lucrative deals and ultra-sophisticated prospective buyers, they don't always transfer well to smaller sales and less prestigious accounts. The fact is, soft-selling is not automatically the best approach to take, nor is it necessarily always welcome.

"You can't measure how fast I hang up the telephone when I've been drawn into a counterfeit conversation with someone asking questions and pretending to be friendly, who then tries to sell me something," cautions psychology professor Ira H. Bernstein (personal communication, April 2, 1999), co-author of *Psychometric Theory* (Nunally, J.C. & Bernstein, I.H., 1994). Bernstein is not alone in that sentiment. There is still a hunger among some segments of the buying public for the direct, straightforward, time efficient sales approach.

Pop-culture chroniclers Jane and Michael Stern attribute the phenomenal financial success of TV infomercials to the fact that they "have restored the lost thrill of salesmanship to shopping" (Stern & Stern, 1992, p. 242). More straightforward "selling" also has found a home among some professional clergy, whose product is eternal salvation rather than vegematic slicing machines or fire-walking seminars. Does it work? Charismatic, fire-and-brimstone factions within Christianity have recently experienced growth that far outstrips that of mainstream denominations, many of which have long ago settled into a warm-and-fuzzy, soft-sell approach to their teachings.

"I want sales training that lets salespeople be salespeople, not psychologists, and encourages them to advocate our products, not apologize for them," says Frank Neese (personal communication, October 19,1995) of Countrywide Mortgage. Neese has an incredibly successful track record setting up and managing highly productive telemarketing organizations in the mortgage banking industry. "To me, soft-selling, regardless of the name it goes by, is a diversion from what selling is about. I have absolutely no use for it. Why would I want to deliberately poison my salespeople?"

In the final analysis, soft-selling simply may have become too clever for its own good. Its architects have attempted to construct a politically correct, hermetically sealed philosophy which pleases everyone, offends no one and raises nary a drop of sweat or a whiff of conflict. Instead, what they've ended up with is a set of tricky gimmicks and win-win platitudes that are plausible without being proven, unassailable without being effective.

Final Irony

At the end of the day, choosing a selling style is up to you. You can stick with tried-and-true traditional selling techniques, or you can embrace the new philosophy of client-centered selling. Or, you can draw from both in whatever proportion adds up to success for you. There is no great ethical issue involved in your choice as long as it is applied honorably. It's your call.

But there is one final point we'd like to make. In the process of expounding soft-sell virtues, a handful of its practitioners have become quite wealthy. That indicates the gurus have definitely been able to make soft-selling work for them. Or have they?

Stop and think. Have you *ever* seen the leading lights of the soft-sell industry pitching their soft-sell training programs by actually using soft-sell techniques? We haven't. In convention speeches, product presentations and video promotions, when it comes to marketing their "revolutionary" training packages, most vendors—surprise!—rely on good old-fashioned product-advocating techniques. Some go even further than that, utilizing the very same methods they disparage as "hard-sell" and manipulative. "Following [my] fundamental rules of selling will lead to sales success faster than any high pressure sales technique" bellows one popular hard-selling soft-sell guru. In similar fashion another states that if you do not use his new *paradigm* of selling, you will soon find yourself on the outside looking in. These are just two examples, but are not isolated ones. Don't take our word for it. Check it out for yourself. Watch and listen to how soft-sell gurus actually pitch their soft-sell training programs. The widespread success of the soft-sell industry is based on traditional, hard sell techniques. And that's the hard truth about soft-selling.

*Ethically grounded salespeople are forthright salespeople. They do not cloak their intent and they do not have to apologize for who they are or what they do — **regardless of their selling style.***

11

Selling With Radical Honesty

The Hard Truth About Soft-Selling maintains that selling is a noble profession, and that salespeople do not inherently dwell on an ethically lower plane simply because they are in sales. It roundly disputes the notion that most salespeople are considered to be untrustworthy, and subsequently, in order to succeed, they must pretend to be doing something other than selling. *The Hard Truth About Soft-Selling* bluntly holds that salespeople should *sell* and that they should do so with pride, purpose and candor. That takes radical honesty and a healthy career identity. Together they complete the ingredients for an authentic, *pro-sales* mindset.

A pro-sales orientation is not associated with or attributable to any particular means, manner or method of selling, and it is not a euphemism for ethics-free manipulation. Sales ethics do not come from some amorphous internal guidance system found in some selling styles but not others. Ethical selling, and more importantly, ethical behavior is the result of honorable *intent*— both on the part of the salesperson and the company represented.

Recommendations, Tips and Suggestions

Here's a quick review of some of the key points developed in *The Hard Truth About Soft-Selling*. It's followed by some tips for current *"pro-sales"* sales professionals and those who wish to be.

- Selling is an integral part of our culture.

- Selling is not inherently unacceptable, wrong or evil, even though some salespeople, like members of any profession, may behave dishonorably.

- Contrary to the preachments of some popular sales training programs, your ethical standing is not the result of the selling style you choose.

- Shunning the so-called "traditional" approach to selling in favor of modern "consultative" selling does not elevate your ethical footing. Ethical behavior is largely the by-product of honorable intent.

- The distorted emphasis on "consulting," "advising," and "negotiating" rather than forthright selling is, in part, a needless camouflage developed to cope with conflicted attitudes about the moral legitimacy of selling.

- The core of the new "client-centered" approach to selling was actually borrowed from the Rogerian ("client-centered") approach to *psychotherapy* popular in the 1950's, which was never intended to increase sales and is, in many respects, the antithesis of selling. Using it to *pretend* to be caring in order to close sales is dishonest.

- The wholesale shift to "soft" selling is largely based on flawed reasoning and knee-jerk reactions. It is not based on adequate, coherent empirical evidence.

- Buyers don't react negatively to selling or to salespeople in general. Buyers react negatively to dishonesty— regardless of the sales approach used.

- Ethically grounded salespeople are forthright salespeople. They do not cloak their intent and they do not have to apologize for who they are or what they do— *regardless of their selling style.*

- Salespeople should be encouraged to adopt a flexible array of styles, not just one, so they can adapt to the communication needs of a variety of prospective buyers.

- Salespeople are expected to sell.

- Salespeople should be allowed to sell.

- Salespeople should be encouraged to adopt a radically honest approach to selling which does not conceal intent, emphasize pretense or result in conflict or shame.

Sales Professionals

Salespeople:

Be open-minded. Ask yourself: "Am I a slave to client-centered selling or am I open to alternative ways of selling?"

Observe. Try to watch various approaches to selling in action. Watch your colleagues, even those you don't agree with.

Learn. Are you doing the hard work only to have your competitors encroach and steal your client? If so, objectively review your approach to selling and watch how other salespeople work— even your competitors.

Join. Consider joining industry or professional sales groups where you have access to both colleagues and competitors. What could you learn over a cup of coffee with a competitor?

Be wary but not cynical. Believe only a portion of the claims you read on the web or hear at industry conventions or sales convocations. (Sales managers should believe even less.)

Disclose. You are a professional salesperson. Buyers expect salespeople to sell them, not befriend them. For some salespeople, especially those indoctrinated into the soft-sell persuasion, forthright disclosure may not be easy. So practice. Rehearse how you might actually sound disclosing that you are in sales in a friendly but honest way to prospective buyers. Try saying something like: *"I'm in sales. Yes, that means I am* *going to try to sell you (your product or service), but I'm also going to try to help you in whatever way you will allow."*

Remember. Clients are opportunities not potential adversaries, or people to be feared.

Edit. Be a discerning consumer. When soft-sell gurus put their hard spin on how you *must* sell, zone out. Daydream. Enjoy a sex fantasy.

Time yourself. Look to your sales cycles. Are they longer than your competitors? That's one of the most obvious signs of rigid soft-selling. Is your selling style artificially extending your sales cycle?

Sales Managers:

Monitor. Watch who you invite to speak to your salespeople. Glib advice without accountability can do more harm than good.

Shop around. Be wary of advice from experts making claims based merely on their own observations and experience.

Chill out. Try to discourage your salespeople from attending those rah-rah sales conventions featuring celebrity non-sales professionals. The distorted emphasis on attitudes and feelings degrades the profession. Think about it. Isn't modern selling about more than "don't worry be happy?" What can your salespeople really learn about selling from a former U.S. president or an ex-soviet leader?

Observe Trainers. Make certain sales trainers behaviorally model genuinely healthy pro-sales attitudes towards selling, rather than conveying mixed messages about the moral acceptability of the sales function. This can be particularly important when sales trainers have little or no sales experience or have been marginal or ineffective producers.

Observe Yourself. What does *your* behavior say to your salespeople? Are you modeling a genuine, pro-sales attitude? Remember, new salespeople will mimic the way you manage your own attitudes about your sales career, which can affect how they manage their attitudes about sales for the rest of their careers.

Prevent. Sponsor regular meetings with your salespeople to frankly and openly discuss their feelings about their sales career. These meetings should be held at least twice monthly and are more efficient than trying to replace salespeople who were unable to become comfortable with their professional identity.

Learn More

Most sales professionals are familiar with all the commercial resources available. There is an unending supply of "breakthrough" books, CDs, speeches, sales workshops, seminars and conventions. Typically, these vary in quality from excellent to brain-dulling exercises in presentational vanity. Surprisingly though, most sales pros are not familiar with one of the best, most accessible, yet typically overlooked resources available. It's your local college or university.

Currently there are approximately 300 professors teaching courses on or directly related to selling. These courses are taught by scholars who are also experienced in sales and sales management, and contain some of the most insightful, credible and up-to-date information available. A few innovative institutions now even offer four-year degree programs in professional selling.

The oldest is the pioneering program at the Center for Professional Selling at Baylor University. Others include William Patterson University, the University of Akron, Ball State University and the University of Houston.

Most colleges and universities currently offer at least some courses related to selling. Though this list is not exhaustive, here are some additional colleges and universities with sales courses and programs: Bowling Green University, Bradley University, Central Missouri State University, University of Central Florida, College of New Jersey, College of St. Catherine, Cornell, Florida State University, Georgia Southern University, Illinois State University, Indiana University, ITESM-Campus Monterrey Mexico,

Kennesaw State University, Loyola Maramount University, Monash University (Australia), Middle Tennessee State University, Minnesota State University, Nicholls State University, Elon University, Northern Illinois University, Purdue, SW Missouri State University, Texas State University, Tuskegee College, University of Texas, University of Wisconsin, University of New Orleans, University of Connecticut and the University of Georgia.

There is another gem salespeople can discover on campus. It's the university level textbooks used to teach selling. You can find them online or in university bookstores. That's because selling is now emerging as an important subject for scholarly research. Formerly elbowed aside by the academic mainstream, it is now finding its own identity as a legitimate and important area of study. The result is a new generation of comprehensive textbooks, high-level articles and white papers. Check them out. One well-written university text on selling can substitute for any number of expensive, mass marketed "how-to" books for salespeople. Here's five of the most popular titles:

- ABCs of Selling (2005), Charles Futrell, McGraw-Hill.

- Relationship Selling & Sales Management (2005), Mark Johnston and Greg Marshall, McGraw-Hill.

- Selling ASAP: Art, Science, Agility, Performance (2004), Eli Jones, Larry Chonko, and Carl Stevens, Thomson Publishing.

- Selling Today: Creating Customer Value (2003), Gerald Manning and Barry Reece, Prentice-Hall.

- Selling: Building Partnerships (2006), Barton A. Weitz, Stephen B. Castleberry, and John F. Tanner Jr., McGraw-Hill.

These books contain some of the latest, most credible information about sales-related subjects available. You can easily find single subject "how-to sell" books and CDs on body language, power selling and other themes. But where else can you find high-level resources covering prospecting and qualifying, overcoming objections, closing sales, managing customer relationships, time management, territory management, goal setting, effective sales management and other important topics without fluff?

REFERENCES

Abelson, R. T. (1995). *Statistics as principled argument.* Hillsdale, NJ: Lawrence Erlbaum Associates.

Abrahams, J. (1999). *The mission statement book.* Berkeley, CA: Ten Speed Press.

Adler, M. J. (1981). *Six great ideas.* New York: Collier Books.

Alessandra & Associates, Inc. (n.d.). *The secret of sales: Matching your selling style with the customer's buying style.* Retrieved May 17, 2005, from http://www.alessandra.com/platinum_members/MatchingYourSellingStyle.asp

Armstrong, R.W. (1992). An empirical investigation of international marketing ethics: problems encountered by Australian firms. *Journal of Business Ethics,* 11, 161-171.

Bagozzi, R.P. (1995). Reflections on relationship marketing in consumer markets. *Journal of the Academy of Marketing Science,* 23, 272-277.

Baker, R. A. (1996). *Mind games.* Amherst, NY: Prometheus Books.

Baker, T.G. (1998). Practice network: Discovering a new construct. *The Society for Industrial and Organizational Psychology TIP Journal,* (35)3.

Beck, A.T. (1976). *Cognitive therapy and the emotional disorders.* New York: International Universities Press.

Beilby Employment Network (n.d.). *Selling styles.* Retrieved May 17, 2005, from http://www.beilby.com.au/BKP/131.aspx

Belizzi, J. (1995). Committing and supervising unethical sales force behavior: the effects of victim gender, victim status, and sales force motivational techniques. *Journal of Personal Selling and Sales Management,* 15, 1-15.

Belizzi, J., & Hite, R.E. (1989). Supervising unethical sales force behavior. *Journal of Marketing,* 53, 36-47.

Bergin, A. E., & Strupp, H.H. (1972). *Changing frontiers in the science of psychotherapy.* New York: Adline-Atherton.

Bernstein, I.H., Dudley, G.W., & Goodson, S.L. (2003, April). *Effects of administration method, gender and country on exaggeration.* Poster session presented at the annual meeting of the Society for Industrial and Organizational Psychology, Orlando, FL.

Beyerstein, B. L. (1990). Brainscams: Neuromythologies of the new age. *International Journal of Mental Health*, 19, 27-36.

Blake, R.R., & Mouton, J.S. (1994). *The managerial grid*. Houston: Gulf Publishing Co.

Bok, S. (1978). *Lying, moral choice in public and private life*. New York: Pantheon Books.

Boles, J., Brashear, T., Bellenger, D., & Barksdale, H., Jr. (2000). Relationship selling behaviors: Antecedents and relationship with performance. *Journal of Business & Industrial Marketing*, 15, 141-153.

Brody, E. J. (1991, March 14). Personal health. *The New York Times*, pp. B8.

Bryant, T.R., & Dudley, G.W. (2005, March). *Exaggeration, gender and selling style*. Poster session presented at the annual meeting of the Southwestern Psychological Association Convention, Memphis, TN.

Campbell, T. W. (1994). *Beware the talking cure*. Boca Raton, LA: Upton Books.

Carnegie, D., Crom, M., & Crom, J.O. (2003). *The sales advantage: How to get it, keep it, and sell more than ever*. New York: Simon & Schuster.

Cattell, R. B., Eber, H.W., & Tatsuoka, M.M. (1970). *Handbook for the sixteen personality factor questionnaire*. Champaign, IL: Institute for Personality and Ability Testing.

Chonko, L. B. & Hunt, S.D. (1985). Ethics and marketing management: An empirical examination. *Journal of Business Research*, 13, 339-353.

Chonko, L.B. & Loe, T.R., (2002). Direct selling ethics at the top: An industry audit and status report. *Journal of Personal Selling & Sales Management*, 22, 87-95.

Chonko, L.B., Tanner, J.F., & Weeks, W.A. (1996). Ethics in salesperson decision making: A synthesis of research approaches and an extension of the scenario method. *Journal of Personal Selling & Sales Management*,16, 35-52.

Churchill, G.A., Ford, N.M., & Walker, O.C. (1990). *Sales force management*. New York: Irwin.

Costa, P.T., Jr., & McCrae, R.R. (1992). *Revised NEO Personality Inventory* (NEO-PI-R) *and NEO Five-Factor Inventory* (NEO-FFI): *Professional manual*. Odessa, FL: Psychological Assessment Resources.

Davies, P. (1995). *Total Confidence*. London: Piatkus Books.

Dawes, R. M. (1994). *House of Cards: Psychology and Psychotherapy Built on Myth*. New York: Free Press.

Dawson, L.E. Jr., Soper, B., & Pettijohn, C.E. (1992). The effects of empathy on salesperson effectiveness. *Psychology & Marketing*, 9, 297-310.

DelVecchio, S.K., Zemanek, J.E., McIntyre, R.P., & Claxton, R.P. (2003). Buyers' perceptions of salesperson tactical approaches. *Journal of Personal Selling and Sales Management*, 23, 39-49.

Direct Selling Association. (n.d.). *Direct selling by the numbers–calendar year 2003*. Retrieved April 13, 2005 from http://www.dsa.org/research/numbers.htm#PEOPLE

Druckmann, D.,& Swets, J.A., (Eds.). (1988). *Enhancing human performance: Issues, theories and techniques*. Washington: National Academy Press.

Dudley, G.W. (1979). *The selling styles profile analysis*. Unpublished manuscript, Behavioral Sciences Research Press.

Dudley, G.W. (1981). The art of recruiting: Going after the blue chips. *Journal of Agent and Management Selection and Development*, 1, 136-149.

Dudley, G. W. (1995). *Call reluctance trend analysis*. Unpublished manuscript, Behavioral Sciences Research Press.

Dudley, G.W., Bryant, T.B., & Bernstein, I.H. (2005, April). *Exaggeration scores and prospectively verifiable sales competencies*. Poster session presented at the annual meeting of the Southwestern Psychological Association Convention, Memphis, TN.

Dudley, G.W., Chonko, L.B. & Tanner, J.F. (2004, April) *Differential diagnosis and incidence of sales call reluctance*. Poster session presented at the annual meeting of the Southwestern Psychological Association Convention, San Antonio, TX.

Dudley, G.W., & Goodson, S.L. (1979). *The call reluctance clinic workbook*. Dallas: Behavioral Sciences Research Press.

Dudley, G.W., & Goodson, S.L. (1980). *Predicting success and failure in life insurance sales*. Unpublished manuscript, Southwestern Life Insurance Company.

Dudley, G. W., & Goodson, S.L. (1981). *Selection resource handbook for the life insurance industry*. Dallas: Behavioral Sciences Research Press.

Dudley, G. W., & Goodson, S.L. (1986). *Fear-Free Prospecting & Self-Promotion Workshop manual*. Dallas: Behavioral Sciences Research Press.

Dudley, G.W., & Goodson, S.L. (1990). *Technical manual for the Sales Preference Questionnare: Call Reluctance Scale*. Dallas: Behavioral Sciences Research Press.

Dudley, G.W., & Goodson, S.L. (1993). *SPQ*Gold: Technical manual*. Dallas: Behavioral Sciences Research Press.

Dudley, G.W., & Goodson, S.L. (1994). *Salespeople or professional visitors? The impact of consultative selling on sales production.* Unpublished manuscript, Behavioral Sciences Research Press.

Dudley, G. W., & Goodson, S.L. (1999). *The psychology of sales call reluctance: earning what you're worth in sales.* Dallas: Behavioral Sciences Research Press.

Dudley, G.W., & Goodson, S.L. (2001, April). *Sales motivation: A multi-nation comparison of what salespeople want.* Poster session presented at the annual meeting of the Southwestern Psychological Association, Houston, TX.

Dudley, G.W., & Goodson, S.L. (2004). *PsychScore technical and administration manual.* Dallas: Behavioral Sciences Research Press.

Dudley, G.W., Goodson, S.L., & Dowe, A.K. (1995). *Attitudes toward prospecting and sales success in the life insurance industry.* Unpublished manuscript, Behavioral Sciences Research Press.

Dudley, G.W., Goodson, S.L., & Field, M.A. (1997, April). *Where in the world can you find an honest salesperson?* Paper presented at the annual meeting of the Southwestern Psychological Association Convention, Fort Worth, TX.

Dunning, D., Meyerowitz, J.A., & Holzberg, A.D. (1989). Ambiguity and self-evaluation: The role of idiosyncratic trait definitions in self-serving assessments of ability. *Journal of Personality and Social Psychology*, 57, 1082-1090.

Ellis, A. (1970). *The essence of rational psychotherapy: A comprehensive approach to treatment.* New York: Institute for Rational Living.

Fenton, J. (1984). *How to sell against competition.* London: Heinemann.

Fox, J. (2000). *How to become a rainmaker.* New York: Hyperion.

Gilbert, J. (2004,October). Smart hiring. *Sales and Marketing Management.* Retrieved June 28, 2005, from http://www.salesandmarketing.com/smm/search/article_display.jsp?vnu_content_id=1000633530

Gitomer, Jeffrey. (2004). *The little red book of selling.* Austin: Bard Press.

Gross, M. L. (1978). *The psychological society.* New York: Simon & Schuster.

Guenzi, P. (2003). Antecedents and consequences of a firm's selling orientation. *European Journal of Marketing*, 37, 706-727.

Haack, S. (1997, November/December). Science, scientism, and anti-science in the age of preposterism. *Skeptical Enquirer*, 60, 37-42.

Hall, J. (Speaker). (2003). *Philosophy of religion* [DVD]. Chantilly, VA: The Teaching Company

Harle, J. R. (1990). *The soft-sell: The role reversal way of selling.* Melbourne: Business Library.

Heinman, S. E., & Sanchez, D. (1998). *The new strategic selling.* New York: Warner Books.

Henderson, V. E. (1992). *What's ethical in business.* New York: McGraw Hill.

Hewitt-Gleeson, M. (1990). *New sell.* Singapore: Singapore Institute of Management.

Honeycutt, E. D., Ford, J. B., & Simintiras, A. C. (2003). *Sales management: A global perspective.* New York: Routledge.

Horgan, J. (1996). *The End of Science.* Reading, MA: Helix Books.

Jackson, D.N. (1994). *Jackson Personality Inventory–Revised: Manual.* London, Ontario: Sigma Assessments Systems, Inc.

Jaramillo, F., Carrillat, F.A., & Locander, W.B. (2003). Starting to solve the method puzzle in salesperson self-report evaluations. *Journal of Personal Selling and Sales Management*, 23, 369-377.

Johnson, S., & Wilson, L., (1984). *The One Minute Sales Person.* New York:William Morrow.

Johnston, K., & Withers, J. (1992). *Relationship selling: Building trust to sell your service.* North Vancouver: Self-Counsel Press.

Jung, C.G. (1971). Psychological types: Volume 6 of the collected works of C. G. Jung. (H.G. Baynes & R.F.C. Hull, Ed. & Trans.). Princeton, N.J: Princeton University Press. (Original work published in 1921)

Kalwani, M.U., & Narayandas, N. (1995). Long term manufacturer-supplier relationships: Do they pay off for supplier firms? *Journal of Marketing*, 59, 1-16.

Keillor, B.D., Parker, R.S., & Pettijohn, C.E. (2000). Relationship-oriented characteristics and individual salesperson performance. *Journal of Business & Industrial Marketing*, 15, 7-22.

Kuhl, J., & Beckmann, J. (Eds.). (1994). *Volition and Personality.* Seattle: Hogrefe & Huber.

LaFollette, M.C. (1992). *Stealing into print: Fraud, plagiarism, and misconduct in scientific publishing.* Berkeley: University of California Press.

Learning International. (1996). *Professional Selling Skills* [Brochure]. Stamford, CT: Author.

Lerner, M. (1995, November/December). Sick of service. *Psychology Today*, 13.

Lindgren, H.C., Byrne, D., & Petrinovich, L. (1968). *Psychology: An introduction to a behavioral science*. New York: John Wiley & Sons.

Lloyd, Simon. (2003, November 9). Selling point. *Business Review Weekly*, 60.

Lilienfeld, S. O. (1996, January/February). EMDR treatment: Less than meets the eye? *Skeptical Enquirer*, 25-31.

MarketWatch. (2003, August 6). *Salespeople: what motivates them to sell? New study shows motivation differs by country*. Retrieved January 27, 2005 from http://www.marketwatch.com/news/newsfinder/archivedArticles.asp?archive=thirdtrue&dist=ArchiveSplash&siteid=mktw&guid=%7B83E2C50F%2D9EC9%2D459F%2D8E37%2D55334594EB39%7D&returnURL=%2Fnews%2Fnewsfinder%2FnewsArticles%2Easp%3Fguid%3D%7B83E2C50F%2D9EC9%2D459F%2D8E37%2D55334594EB39%7D%26siteid%3Dmktw%26archive%3Dthirdtrue

Marshall, G.W. (1992). The impact of territory difficulty and self versus other ratings on managerial evaluations of sales personnel. *Journal of Personal Selling and Sales Management*, 22. 35-47.

Mende, B. (2004). *Employers crack down on candidates who lie*. Retrieved June 14, 2005, from http://www.careerjournal.com/jobhunting/resumes/20020606-mende.html

Merrill, D. & Reid, R. (1981). *Personal styles and effective performance*. Radnor, PA: Chilton.

Miller, R.B., & Williams, G.A. (2004). *The five paths to persuasion: The art of selling your message*. New York: Warner Business Books.

Moynahan, J. E. (Ed.). (1991). *The sales compensation handbook*. New York: AMACOM.

Myers, I.B., McCaulley, M.H., Quenk, N.L., & Hammer, A.L. (1998). *Manual: A guide to the development and use of the Myers-Briggs Type Indicator*. Palo Alto, CA: Consulting Psychologists Press.

Nunally, J.C., & Bernstein, I. H. (1994). *Psychometric theory*. New York: McGraw-Hill, Inc.

Nylen, R. (1996, May). Do we need sales certification? *Selling*, 69-70.

Onsman, H. (2005, April 4). Busted: neuro-babble. *The Australian Financial Review*, pp. 16.

Park, J., & Holloway, B.B. (2003). Adaptive selling behavior revisited: An empirical examination of learning orientation, sales performance, and job satisfaction. *Journal of Personal Selling and Sales Management*, 23, 239-251.

Parinello, A. (1999). *Selling to VITO*. Avon, MA: Adams Media.

Plotkin, D. N. (1995). *Selling to humans: A new approach to exchange*. Cotati, CA: Influence Training Systems.

Porter, S.S., Wiener, J.L., & Frankwick, G.L. (2003). The moderating effect of selling situation on the adaptive selling strategy-selling effectiveness relationship. *Journal of Business Research*, 56, 275-281.

Reed, R. (1996, December/January). Consumers Want Service. *Crain's Chicago Business.*

Rogers, C. (1942). *Counseling and psychotherapy.* Boston: Houghton Mifflin.

Rogers, C. (1951). *Client centered therapy.* Boston: Houghton Mifflin.

Sadgrove, R. (1994). *Seductive Selling.* London: Kogan.

Sales Training and Results, Inc. (n.d.). *Selling styles.* Retrieved May 17, 2005, from http://www.salestrainingandresults.com/art_sellingstyles.html

Schneider, J. (1990). *The feel of success in selling.* Englewood Cliffs, NJ: Prentice-Hall.

Shapiro, E. H. Jr., Schwartz, C.E., & and Astin, J.A. (1996). Controlling ourselves, controlling our world: Psychology's role in understanding positive and negative consequences of seeking and gaining control. *American Psychologist*, 51, 1213-1230.

Shapiro, E.C. (1995). *Fad surfing in the boardroom.* New York: Addison-Wesley.

Stengel, R. (2000). *You're too kind.* New York: Simon & Schuster.

Stern, J., & S. Stern. (1992). *The encyclopedia of popular culture.* New York: HarperPerennial.

Strazewski, L. (1996, April). Incentives tap customer bliss. *Crain's Chicago Business.*

Strout, E. (2001, February). Are your salespeople ripping you off? *Sales and Marketing Management*, 57-62.

Tabak, L. (1997, December/January). If Your goal Is success, don't consult these gurus. *Fast Company*, p. 40.

Tack, A. (1993). *How to increase your sales to industry.* London: Mandarin Paperbacks.

Tanner, J.F. (1994). Adaptive selling at trade shows. *Journal of Personal Selling and Sales Management*, 14, 15-23.

Tanner, J.F., & Dudley, G.W. (2003, November). *International differences: Examining two assumptions about selling.* Paper presented at the meeting of the Society for Marketing Advances, New Orleans, LA.

Technology, putting it to the test, human resources. (1997, January). *Inc. Magazine.*

Thomas, R. (1985). *Advanced lie detection techniques.* Austin, Texas: Ralph Thomas.

Thoresen, C.J., Bradley, J.C., Bliese, P.D., & Thoresen, J.D. (2004). The big five personality traits and individual job performance growth trajectories in maintenance and transitional job stages. *Journal of Applied Psychology*, 89, 835-853.

Tracy, B. (1993). *Advanced Selling Strategies*. New York: Fireside.

Trevino, L.K., & Youngblood, S.A. (1990). Bad apples in bad barrels: A causal analysis of ethical decision-making behavior. *Journal of Applied Psychology*, 75, 378-385.

United States Census Bureau (2004). *Occupational employment and wages–May, 2004: Sales and related occupations*. Retrieved April 12, 2005 from http://www.bls.gov/oes/current/oes410000.htm

Vinchur, A.J., Schippmann, J.S., Switzer, F.S., & Roth, P.L. (1998). A meta-analytic review of predictors of job performance for salespeople. *Journal of Applied Psychology*, 83, 586-597.

Wagner, J.A., Klein, N.M., & Keith, J.E. (2003). Buyer-seller relationships and selling effectiveness: The moderating influence of buyer expertise and product competitive position. *Journal of Business Research*, 56, 295-302.

Walsh, S.M. (2004). Call reluctance: The dark side of professional selling? *Southern Business Review Statesboro*, 29, 23-32.

Weitz, B. A., Castleberry, S.B., & Tanner, J.F. (2004). *Selling: Building partnerships*. Boston: McGraw Hill Irwin.

Wenschlag, R. (1987). *The versatile salesperson: Selling the way your customer wants to buy*. New York: John Wiley & Sons.

Willingham, R. (1987). *Integrity selling*. New York: Doubleday.

Wilson, L. (1997). *Stop selling, start partnering*. New York: John Wiley & Sons.

Wilson Learning. (2001). *The counselor salesperson*. Retrieved September 28, 2004, from http://portalcenter.wilsonlearning.com/pls/portal/docs/page/wlc_web_site/file_holder/44574_csp_overview.pdf

Yahoo!Finance: U.K. & Ireland. (2003, February 11). *What motivates UK salespeople to sell? New university study shows sales motivation differs by country*. Retrieved January 27, 2005, from http://uk.finance.yahoo.com/

LIST OF FIGURES

INDEX

INFORMATION

For more information about ongoing sales research at
Behavioral Sciences Research Press:

http://www.bsrpinc.com/research/papers.htm

For information about the pioneering Center for Professional
Selling at Baylor University:

http://www.baylor.edu/business/selling

ABOUT THE AUTHORS

George W. Dudley

Noted behavioral scientist and author, George W. Dudley, has degrees in research psychology from Baylor University and the University of North Texas. He began working with psychological assessments while serving in the U.S. Marine Corps, and for many years directed the Field Testing & Research department of a Fortune 500 financial services company. His ground-breaking studies of sales call reluctance, begun in the mid 1970's, have been featured in popular and professional media including CNN, The Financial Times of London, The Australian, European Association for Behavioural and Cognitive Therapies and the Society for Industrial and Organizational Psychology. He is the principle author of the seminal textbook, *The Psychology of Sales Call Reluctance*, an international best seller for over 15 years. A gifted teacher, he has been a featured platform speaker at many industry and professional conventions including the Million Dollar Roundtable and the Singapore Association of Life Underwriters. His scientific studies such as *"Where In the World Can You Find An Honest Salesperson?"* and *"What Really Motivates Salespeople: A Multi-Nation Comparison"* have generated worldwide interest. He is married and lives in the Dallas area with his wife, scientist Carol A. Dudley, who has published research in physiology and genetics.

John F. (Jeff) Tanner, Jr.

John F. (Jeff) Tanner Jr., Ph.D., is professor of marketing and the research director for Baylor University's Center for Professional Selling. Prior to entering academia, he spent eight years in marketing and sales with Rockwell International and Xerox® Corporation. He is the author or co-author of numerous published research papers related to salespeople and their profession. He is a leading expert in Customer Relationship Management and is frequently invited to lecture on a range of subjects including effective exhibit marketing, modern sales selection, and global sales performance issues. His curriculum design efforts have won national acclaim, including the Southwest Business Dean's Innovation Award. Dr. Tanner is co-author of *Selling: Building Partnerships* one of the most popular university level textbooks on professional selling. Internationally noted, Dr. Tanner has taught account management and sales courses to executives and business schools in many countries including France, Trinidad, Canada, Mexico and India. Dr. Tanner lives on a farm in Waco, Texas where he breeds horses and writes a column on sales management issues for *Sales and Marketing Strategies & News*.